Postcolonial Borderlands

Postcolonial Borderlands: Orality and Irish Traveller Writing

By

Christine Walsh (Mícheál Ó hAodha, editor)

Cambridge Scholars Publishing

Postcolonial Borderlands: Orality and Irish Traveller Writing,
by Christine Walsh (Mícheál Ó hAodha, editor)

This book first published 2008 by

Cambridge Scholars Publishing

15 Angerton Gardens, Newcastle, NE5 2JA, UK

British Library Cataloguing in Publication Data
A catalogue record for this book is available from the British Library

ISBN (10): 1-84718-449-9, ISBN (13): 9781847184498

To my four sons who never cease to inspire me

"Most of what I know comes from listening to tales around the camp-fire".
—Seán Maher 1972, 113

Table of Contents

PREFACE

The Irish Travellers, a traditionally nomadic people indigenous to Ireland, have suffered marginalization and discrimination within modern Ireland. This volume, informed by Michel Foucault's musings on the struggles for power within the modern nation, explores the history of colonialism as an unresolved trauma that has contributed to the persecution of Travellers in Ireland. In addition to the history of systemic racism exercised against them, Travellers' traditionally oral culture has meant that they have been excluded from many educational institutions. As a consequence the majority of Traveller autobiographies (most published within the last twenty years) have been "spoken" works such as Traveller activist Nan Joyce's *My Life on the Road* (1985, 2000), one of two longer autobiographies focused on in this volume. Joyce's direct style approaches language as a primarily social interaction, one which is characteristic of the orality she employs to respond to the negative representations of Travellers within the dominant culture. Although Seán Maher's more literary memoir, *The Road to God Knows Where* (1972, 1998), reflects his formal education, his focus remains on storytelling as he writes to preserve Traveller traditions which he views as imperilled. Both writers present worldviews that challenge not only the more literary expectations of the presumed non-Traveller reader, but also the academic 'othering' that delegitimizes knowledge derived from orality and ultimately, the rational materialism that validates the homogenizing and normalizing impulses which regulate the modern nation. By re-presenting official versions of history in narratives that include Travellers as active participants, Joyce and Maher reveal the role of storytelling in creating a sense of nationhood even as they write to construct legitimate places of belonging for Travellers within the Irish nation.

ACKNOWLEDGEMENTS

I would like to thank my thesis advisor, Professor Michael Kenneally for all of the years he has encouraged me in my studies. In writing this volume, he allowed me the freedom to explore my ideas but managed always to bring me back to focus. I would also like to extend gratitude to my two readers, Professor Bina Freiwald for her appreciation and support of my efforts, and Professor Andre Furlani whose meticulous reading and corrections helped propel my theorisation towards a more refined analysis. Finally, I would like to thank Mícheál Ó hAodha who, with the support of the Traveller / Migration Access Initiative, was instrumental in bringing this book to fruition.

Cover photo is of a model of a Traveller's caravan (trailer) made by Irish artist, Seamus Nolan. Nolan graduated from National College of Art and Design in Dublin, Ireland with a first class honours degree in sculpture in 2004. Nolan was the winner of the 2006 Emerging Visual Artist Award. He has recently been awarded a studio placement by Independent Artists' Studios in Temple Bar, and a residency at the Irish Museum of Modern Art. He was a recipient of an Irish Arts Council bursary in both 2006 and 2007.

INTRODUCTION

The Travellers are a traditionally nomadic minority group indigenous to Ireland. In former days, they travelled the countryside in horse-drawn caravans, wagons and tents. Those Travellers who are still nomadic or semi-nomadic in the present today are more likely to be pulling caravans (frequently referred to as "trailers" by Travellers) behind their vans or cars. Decades of settlement and overtly-assimilationist policies have ensured that well over half of all Travellers living in Ireland live more sedentary or "settled" lives for the major part of the year.

The reasons that Travellers have been marginalized and ostracised within Ireland are complex and long-standing. In focusing on two autobiographical works by Traveller writers, this volume reveals the legacy of colonialism as a strong contributory factor, in addition to the prevailing perception of nomadism as a threat to sedentary values that Robbie McVeigh (1997) identifies as "anti-nomadism". Dominant discourses tended to erase Travellers from the mythologies of nationhood that fortified nationalist aspirations and, later, subsequent to the formation of an independent state, continued to espouse a definition of Irishness that promoted an ostensible homogeneity. In her autobiography, *My Life on the Road* (1985, 2000), community activist Nan Joyce reaches out to (an assumed) non-Traveller[1] Irish audience, arguing for a meaningful place for Travellers within contemporary Irish society. She portrays Travellers as patriotic Irish citizens who simultaneously maintain their difference as a separate people through their long-established and unique culture within Ireland and abroad. While Joyce's dialogic style differs greatly from the more literary style of Seán Maher's memoir, *The Road to God Knows Where* (1972, 1998), and while the two works represent politically divergent views, both serve to write Traveller culture back into the Irish historical landscape.

---

[1] Although Joyce refers to non-Travellers as "settled", with approximately half of the Traveller population now settled in permanent housing for at least part of the year, this volume employs the term non-Traveller. Joyce and other Travellers also sometimes refer to non-Travellers as "country people". Maher's text often uses the term "gentry", a term which accentuates class differences and conveys a sense of privilege as associated with the landowning class.

Irish Government policies have previously attempted to both contain and control the perceived recalcitrance of Travellers' nomadic lifestyle. By creatively redefining Irishness and the place of Travellers within the nation, however, Joyce and Maher's texts represent the kind of responsive discourse that Michel Foucault (1988) has referred to as "a stumbling-block, a point of resistance and a starting point for an opposing strategy" (Foucault 1988, 101). Crucial to an informed reading of Traveller-produced writing is an awareness of the subtlety and pervasiveness whereby privileged discourses have both excluded and discredited particular types of knowledge. The ways in which oral cultures perceive the world tend to be dismissed within literate cultures as "naïve". This attitude confirms Foucault's finding that certain kinds of knowledge are "subjugated" — de-legitimized because they are deemed as "inadequate to their task or insufficiently elaborated", and are therefore "located low down on the hierarchy, beneath the required level of cognition or scientificity" (Foucault 1980, 82). Joyce and Maher's autobiographies challenge the assumptions whereby certain kinds of knowledge are discredited. In proposing the legitimacy of oral history, for example, they strike at the rationale that premised the legitimation of decades-long and officially sanctioned settlement policies – the latter often termed "re-settlement". At the same time, through the process of telling their stories (paradoxically in written form), these writers ensure the preservation of cultural memory and are a catalyst for resistance against ongoing assimilationist pressures. Their texts corroborate Leigh Gilmore's (1994) assertion that "writing an autobiography can be a political act because it asserts the right to speak rather than to be spoken for" (1994, 40).

Homi Bhabha (1994) cites "'literacy'" amongst the "'key'" homogenising impulses in the modern nation-state (Bhabha citing Gellner, 1994, 142); oral forms represent a counterpoint to these homogenizing, unifying trends. While narratives privileged within a nation enjoy official recognition in public ceremonies, school curricula etc., tangential versions retain cultural tenability and even vitality by employing more covert methods of dissemination through oral expressions that Gibbons (1996) refers to as "fugitive and endangered cultural forms" (1996, 145). These include the traditional Traveller (Cant) songs Maher performs before his astonished classmates and the stories he relates[2]. Storytelling is flexible,

---

[2] Residual orality provided an important functional role as Joyce asserts in an anecdote which describes one offshoot of Traveller nomadic economic activity – i.e., the dissemination of information, not only between Travellers, but also between the Traveller and settled communities. In the Ireland of her youth, Joyce describes the isolation of some of their rural clients:

responsive to the past but adaptive to present circumstances in ways that cannot be restrained. The recalcitrance of oral cultures to assimilation has therefore been perceived as a fundamental obstacle to the "unifying" imperatives of modernity.

There are a number of crucial differences between literary practices and preoccupations, and the more concrete concerns of orality. Orality, as Walter Ong (1967, 1991) points out, is "always embedded in non-verbal existence" (1991, 160). Literacy, on the other hand, permits more abstract and analytical thinking because ideas can be recorded and returned to, re-examined, reflected on and modified. However, the abstracting tendency that is common to literate thinking can become an oppressive instrument when it questions the validity of the experiential vocabularies most apt to be available to more marginalized people. Certain academic paradigms including those postmodernist discourses which have questioned the validity of "lived experience" as a valid epistemology because it is socially mediated (Cavallaro 2001, 40), for example, have the effect of duplicating exclusionary practices, further marginalizing already marginalized people. As Shari Stone-Mediatore (2003) explains, "the viewpoints of people who have been the most socially and culturally marginalized are not presented in 'theories,' in the standard sense of the term, but in engaged, creative, community-situated 'stories'" (2003, 163). These modes of expression based on life experience are often the only ones available to people like Travellers who have been "excluded from official knowledge-producing institutions"[3] (Stone-Mediatore 2003, 163). To dismiss the Traveller point of view because certain types of "experience" are a non-privileged form of knowledge effectively silences marginalized people by denying the legitimacy of less theoretical modes of discourse.

> If they were living on the side of a mountain, or in a real lonely place, they mightn't get to the town for six months and they loved to see the travellers coming so that they could get their pots and kettles mended and buy little things. In those days the half-doors would all be open. You'd look in across the door and ask the woman did she want anything and she'd ask you in to have a cup of tea. She'd say, 'Now, tell us all the news. What's happening in Belfast?'
>
> So we were sort of newspapers and radios as well as everything else. (Joyce 2000, 3)

[3] Lack of access to formal education is a recurring theme in Traveller autobiographies, including Joyce's. Not only do forced relocations, "shifting" by authorities mean removing children from school, but Traveller accounts also relate the forms of hostility Traveller students may endure – including taunts by fellow students, and insensitivity or outright segregation by teachers etc.

Autobiography tends for the most part to be largely influenced by realism and uses representations to signify an individual's life and even an inner "self" and is closely linked to the construction of self-identity since both rely on a sense of continuity achieved through memory. As Rakow and Wackwitz (2004) point out, the self "is a composite, remembered self" (Rakow and Wackwitz citing Susannah Radstone 2004, 173). The process of remembering "rais[es] questions about what we wish to remember" (Rakow and Wackwitz 2004, 173) since this, by implication, also always involves what we choose to forget. As Michel de Certeau (1988) outlines in his analysis of history (which aptly applies to autobiography to the degree that the latter represents an individual's "history making"), the process of "selection between what can be *understood* and what must be *forgotten* in order to obtain the representation of a present intelligibility" (de Certeau 1988, 4) also creates *absences*. In the autobiographical text, certainly in Joyce's text, such absences tend to be represented as silences so that, what is not said sometimes resonates with a more profound meaning. Trauma also may be a major obstacle to remembering, but again, such silences often resonate in a text. Forgetting, in order to remember, applies to the formation of any cultural or historical text and not just autobiography since such undertones contain cultural meaning — they represent not only the unspeakable, but also, being a kind of self-regulating collective censorship, the unthinkable.

This thesis aligns itself with the theoretic approach of Richard Dyer (1993) in presuming that while representations are not without limitations, they are "also what makes saying possible at all" (Dyer 1993, 2). Dyer (1993) recognizes that dominant cultures can and do use representations of marginalized groups in ways that justify oppressive practices (Dyer 1993, 1), but subjugated peoples can (and do) represent themselves in creative ways that resist such definitions. Joyce's (2000) occasionally direct refutations of negative beliefs propagated in the non-Traveller community regarding Travellers reveal that she understands "conflicts over representations are struggles over meaning" (Rakow and Wackwitz 2004, 172), and that received beliefs can be changed (Rakow and Wackwitz 2004, 174). Joyce's belief that ignorance, or "a fear of the unknown" (Joyce 2000, 118), is often the root cause of racism is a strong motivating factor in her writing. However, Joyce's text also reveals some of the challenges of working within and responding to the values and representations of a dominant culture. (These will be examined in Part I.)

Joyce's text evinces confidence in the ability of language to communicate, a relationship with language tied to the fact that oral interactions naturally imply a speaker and a receiver, or "narrator and addressee" as Sidonie Smith and Julia Watson (2001) describe the interrelation between autobiographer and reader, a relationship "that is fundamental to autobiographical acts and the kinds of intersubjective truth they construct" (Smith and Watson 2001, 69). (Smith and Watson's observation suggests a parallel between autobiography and speech.) The tendency of both Maher (1998) and Joyce (2000) to view subjectivity as more communal than individualistic reflects the inherent sociality of the spoken word. As Ong (1967, 1991) remarks, "Oral communication unites people in groups" (Ong 1991, 69). Both autobiographies downplay individualism in favour of more communal conceptions of self, diverging from the Cartesian concept of an interior, isolated Self. Ong attributes the invention of the Cartesian model to literacy because "writing and reading are solitary activities that throw the psyche back on itself" (Ong 1991, 69). He proposes that widespread literacy and the availability of written materials on a global level have both changed the way people interact, creating an isolating effect that preceded theories that hypothesized more individualistic paradigms[4]. Descartes privatized thought by stressing the "logic of personal enquiry", a move that "ousted … the art of discourse", a collaborative intellectual activity maintained among institutions of learning until Descartes revolutionized "the art of thinking [as an] isolated intellectual activity" (Ong 1967, 63). This shift from orality to literacy was not instantaneous. Learning techniques emphasized dialectic and rhetoric "well through the Renaissance" (Ong 1967, 293). However, Ong postulates that the invention of the printing press and ready access to print culture "intensified the inwardness" of human thought (Ong 1991, 153).

While there are probably very few cultures now in existence which can be identified as "primary oral cultures" (Ong 1991, 31) – i.e. cultures that consider words (as sounds) to be primary and have never been exposed to the theoretics of inscribing languages – many cultures nevertheless remain intricately connected to their oral heritage. Orality has also deeply influenced the development of Western literacy, although this fact is seldom acknowledged today. Some of Western culture's seminal texts, the *Pentateuch* and Homer's *Iliad*, for example, were oral compositions prior to being written down. Traces of orality continue to resonate like an after-touch in the form of various stylistic idiosyncrasies as evidenced in these texts. Similarly, strong traces of Celtic folktales, popular beliefs, legends and myths resonate even within a modern culture such as Ireland's, to some extent the same forms which were adopted and adapted by the

[4] In the same way as the multiplicity of electronic communications devices will undoubtedly shape present-day generations.

Anglo-Irish Literary Revival at the turn of the century (see Helleiner). While Ong (1967, 1991) refers to orality and literacy as "polarities" (Ong, 1991, 157) on more than one occasion, the sub-text of his oeuvre suggests that orality and literacy are not mutually exclusive. In actual fact, he proposes that "*[l]'écriture* and orality are both 'privileged'" (Ong 1991, 169), since each of these modes can inform one another. The continuing development of electronic media has seen the spoken word combined with literary variants and types in formats such as text messaging – the latter essentially comprising a "conversation" constructed through non-grammatical syntax and truncations[5]. Digital communications are again creating a revolution, transforming interpersonal and informational exchange to such a degree that the contemporary world is arguably evolving into a secondary oral / secondary literate culture (Fowler 2006). While the constraints of this volume mean that there is no space here for the exploration of these shifting hybrids, this volume presupposes the view that the dichotomization of orality / literacy is a construct that may in itself have derived from the Western dialectic tradition[6], one where an individual argued against an opponent (sometimes imaginary, sometimes in attendance) in order to affirm or "win" one's position (Ong 1991, 111). "[T]he 'art' of rhetoric" developed an "agonistic dynamics" that "situate[d] knowledge within a context of struggle" (Ong 1991, 44, 45), a tendency evident in Joyce's text where she addresses an imagined audience / reader in order to convince. In addition to the assumption of an imagined listener, Joyce's emphasis on "social" issues such as housing, in addition to human inter-relations coincides with the practical preoccupations of an orality that remains grounded in lived relations.

Since the spoken word is also an action (Ong 1991, 31, 32), a passing instant in time that cannot be retrieved, mnemonic devices are a characteristic structural aspect of the oral style - including the use of rhyme, metre and alliteration (Ong 1991, 34). Formulaic language such as the use of epithets (Ong 1991, 38) provides a shorthand of meanings and character "types" often already familiar to the audience[7]. Repetitions serve as memory aids, reminding both the speaker and the audience of what has

---

[5] Although he was writing prior to the era of personal computers, Ong acknowledges this in *The Presence of the Word: Some Prolegomena for Cultural and Religious History*. New Haven & London: Yale UP (1967, 9).

[6] See Habermas, *The Philosophical Discourse of Modernity*, 1987.

[7] As Dyer (1993) has made clear, more literate societies also call upon a battery of cultural codes as embedded in the collective consciousness so as to be received uncritically. Political rhetoric in addition to other public forums such as advertising are but examples of language as mutually understood cultural meanings.

gone before. Ong regards the "redundancy" characteristic of oral presentations as more "natural" than "[s]parsely linear or analytic thought and speech" (Ong 1991, 40) which developed when the technology of writing freed the mind from the necessity of having to commit everything to memory. Orality tends to be less grammatically rigorous given that so much of the meaning is imparted through non-verbal means, as explained by Ong (1991): "Written discourse develops more elaborate and fixed grammar … because … meaning … is more dependent … upon linguistic structure" (Ong 1991, 38).

The oral influence evident in Joyce's *My Life on the Road* is, in part, a direct consequence of the fact that its narrative was spoken into a tape recorder and then transcribed into text form by the book's editor, Anna Farmar. The structure of the entire text, its additions from other sources – i.e. newspaper articles, Ewan MacColl's "The Moving-on Song", traditional verse-poems etc. – must therefore be considered as collaborative choices. In personal correspondence, Farmar explained the nature of their collaborative process: "Nan spoke about her life, sometimes prompted by me, sometimes I would ask her to clarify something, but on the whole she just talked (not always in chronological sequence!)"[8]. Farmar's comments suggest that arranging the anecdotes into as close a chronological narrative as possible was a challenging task. This is not particularly surprising given that there is a tendency to assign less importance to linearity in oral compositions. Farmar reworked Joyce's recorded anecdotes, minimizing the characteristic repetitions and circularity of the oral process thereby reshaping the spoken word into a more linear and more literary style. Farmar's approach appears a very appropriate one given that Joyce communicates her life story in order to bring to light a range of larger issues which affect her as an individual but which also affect Travellers as a group. For a work such as hers, which indicates as its expressed purpose the promotion of both political and social change, Farmar's decision to reduce redundancy, fashioning a tenuous chronology of sometimes disparate anecdotes, probably best succeeds in conveying Joyce's intentions. Working in tandem with this socio-political process was a discourse whereby Farmar attempted to ensure that "[the work] should be mediated as little as possible"[9]. Farmar successfully retains the unique "voice" that is Nan Joyce's, though the non-text based elements of Joyce's delivery – i.e. laughter, voice inflections or physical gestures – are lost in the process. In order to

---

[8] Email received from Anna Farmar, Dec. 13, 2005, in answer to my queries on the collaborative process.

[9] Personal correspondence (See endnote 8 above.)

compensate for this loss, perhaps, and in an attempt to preserve the sound of Joyce's speech, Farmar retains some colloquialisms such as "afeard" for "afraid", "usen't to" for "did not used to" in the text. "Ungrammatical" elements, such as the liberal use of commas to connect independent clauses in the written text also serve to duplicate the pauses for breath of the speaking voice. The frequency of run-on sentences in the text simulates the rapidity with which thoughts translate into words, thereby lending support to Ong's observation that speech reflects "additive" thought patterns. Not only do oral forms tend to link ideas through the use of such constructions as "and" (Ong 1991, 37), but these "aggregative" groupings also tend to organize ideas through temporal or relational (as opposed to) sequential or logical correspondences (Ong 1991, 38). Aggregation also reflects a worldview that seeks unity – a manner of interpreting the world that will be examined in greater detail later in this volume[10].

Traveller: The Genesis of an Autobiography

Nan Joyce was born to nomadic Travellers in 1940, the second of ten children, one of whom died in infancy. Her autobiography, originally entitled *Traveller*, and first published in 1985, can be (informally) divided into two halves. The first half of her book comprises a range of sometimes-unconnected anecdotes which depict an idyllic childhood, memories of her family life at this juncture, some happy recollections of her father for whom she had great admiration. From a life where all of their needs were met by their attentive parents, the family fell on "hard times" after their father was killed in police custody when Joyce was only twelve years old. With nine children to care for, including a newborn baby, and faced with a jail sentence because she was unable to pay fines for illegal camping, her mother and another woman – (in desperation) stole some scrap so as to generate some badly-needed income. The women were caught however and imprisoned for one year. For the next twelve months, the children had to survive on their own. The care of six younger siblings fell to twelve-year-old Nan, her older sister Kathleen, aged fourteen, and their younger brother, Willie, who was only ten. Necessity dictated that the family employed every means of subsistence survival including begging, stealing food and trading in scrap. Joyce's account of these months intersperses humorous anecdotes within a Dickensian

[10] See Part III of this volume.

scenario – i.e. unsupervised children living in very impoverished circumstances on the margins of a seemingly indifferent society[11]. Subsequent to her mother's release, the narrative skips forward a few years to when, at the age of sixteen, Joyce marries and starts her own family.

Although she experienced periods of severe deprivation in her childhood, Joyce's reminiscences from this period are full of a buoyant and (sometimes) "dark" humour. The second half of the book, which concerns Joyce's adult life, represents a marked change in tone, however. Now, the focus moves almost exclusively onto the question of daily survival including such primal needs as health, education and housing. The difference between childhood and adulthood is a marked one. While her childhood also meant that she bore the burden of many adult responsibilities, it was nonetheless a temporary, if very difficult situation. As an adult with children of her own, her family's troubles fall squarely on her shoulders.

Joyce's emphasis on the public sphere in the second half of the book, including the struggles on behalf of her family that lead to her socio-political activism, allows her personal life to remain in the background. Her evasion of any detailed discussion on the question of individual relations may reflect her characteristic personal reticence, or may also be indicative of a preference to foreground issues that affect not just her, but the Traveller community in general.

This conflict between her inclination to speak more frankly and her reticence in divulging those personal details that she would consider an invasion of her marital and family spheres ensures a narrative tone that is both straightforward and reticent at the same time. Certain subjects are not broached at all. She rarely identifies her own personal feelings, for example, although the intuitive reader may yet gain an understanding of some of her emotions. Her relationship with her husband is a subject that remains private and thereby represents a "silence" within the text. Joyce often appears alone when in situations of direst need as if circumstances have dictated that she has to cope with such difficulties alone. The emphasis on the public sphere that is reflective of the second half of the book represents what Gilmore (1994) identifies as a "masculinist" (1994, 45) approach to the text, Gilmore asserting that male autobiographers tend to place greater emphasis on the public life as opposed to the private life. To the degree that this may be true, Joyce differs from a more

[11] Although the system was obviously negligent, the children also were so fearful of being taken in by authorities, they used every tactic to avoid detection. Their aversion underlines the suspicion with which they viewed figures of authority, a distrust not altogether unjustified.

individualistic narrative model. She does not emphasize to any great extent events which are the consequence of individual achievement and instead, she highlights her concern for others, including her family, thereby expressing a representation of "the self in relation to others" (Gilmore 1994, 77) that has been typical of much female autobiography. Perhaps because she wishes to foreground certain issues, Joyce (2000) tends to focus on events rather than their psychological or emotional effect on her as an individual. Recurring patterns or themes emerge throughout her narrative including the unremitting struggle to find adequate shelter and the problems of ill-health that affect Travellers. Traveller children, in particular, suffer frequent health problems, often as a direct result of their hazardous and unhealthy surroundings. These difficulties are compounded by a frequent and unremitting harassment on the part of the local authorities who regularly implement forced evictions, thereby creating more instability for the Traveller families. While Joyce resists the bullying attitude of many local officials earlier on, the death of her first grandchild as a direct consequence of poor housing – the toddler probably contracted the meningitis that killed her from rats infesting their camp environment – brings a stronger focus and outspokenness to her activism and she begins to take on an enhanced leadership role within the community.

The almost total absence of psychological self-reflexivity that is characteristic of Joyce's narrative reflects the predisposition of oral thought not to delve into abstract analysis. Joyce does discuss certain issues as relating to the class struggle, analyses that exhibit certain analogies with Marxist paradigms and theoretical frameworks, as outlined in previous work in advocacy-type writing by members of marginal and "outsider" groups. Her aversion to self-analysis may arguably represent a tacit rejection of the self-indulgent, "bourgeois" sensibilities that are typical of literature produced under the influence of Freudian-type psychoanalysis. Joyce exhibits a greater concern for community instead, one which demands an externalizing impetus that addresses a presumed non-Traveller audience / reader. This suggests that writing oneself into the national discourse is never a strictly self-reflexive proposition. Whether for this reason, or for a combination of reasons, Joyce rarely divulges her own private thoughts or feelings.

Despite this reticence, a strong sense of self-identity emerges, one encompassing a firm attachment to familial relations. Joyce defines herself in relation to others, a network that enlarges to embrace a wider range of networks and communities. Mary G. Mason (1988) was one of the first autobiography theorists to notice a tendency among women autobiographers to define themselves in terms of "alterity" (1988, 41). This self-perception, one which consciously acknowledges the involvement and influence of close personal kin - as an extension of self - runs contrary to the individualism that is characteristic of the Cartesian model outlined above. Cruikshank (1994, 1998), whose research was based amongst societies[12] still steeped in oral traditions, argues that within these social structures, knowledge itself is "relational" and should be regarded "more like a verb than a noun" (1998, 70). The relationality that is characteristic of these oral societies becomes particularly evident in the transmission of knowledge through storytelling.

Seán Maher's *The Road to God Knows Where*: Autobiography as a Communal Story

In Seán Maher's *The Road to God Knows Where* (1972, 1998), the prominence given to storytelling suggests that memory is collective and that an individual's identity develops through a cultural identity that is communal in nature. In Maher (1998), the importance of human relations is frequently emphasized by its absence. Life on the road means a constantly changing environment where social relations also encompass sometimes-long periods of separation. This instability creates a profound sense of loneliness in young Seán, a loneliness which is intensified by a troubled family life. Maher, who goes by the pseudonym Seán Devine in the text, intertwines storytelling with real-life events to such an extent that the line between the fictional and the factual, and the ordinary and the uncanny, frequently blurs. Lanters (2005) argues that this name change is indicative of "a slightly fictionalized account of his life" (2005, 26), but it is not clear to what extent this is true. Maher does employ novel-type techniques including long and detailed conversations that he would most certainly not have been able to remember verbatim. He also includes various dialogues between people such as his parents where he, himself, is absent, without indicating how he has come by this information. Alternatively, this use of a fictional name may help create the emotional distance between the writer / narrator Maher and the character that is Seán. Transposing the wretched aspects of his childhood onto this Seán Devine

[12] Cruikshank (1998) is referring here to hunter-gatherer societies, but the observation can also be extended to include those oral-based societies, including small-scale agrarian societies, where knowledge tends to be steeped primarily in survival issues, the practical aspects of daily life, the fluctuating demands of seasonal cycles etc. This is not to suggest that such societies have no cultural life, but rather that their cultural activities will always reflect this primary relation with the nonhuman world, to some degree.

character permits Maher the writer to recall memories that are both painful and suppressed.

Despite Maher's strong emphasis on storytelling, there is a less accidental impression to his anecdotes than there is in the first half of *My Life on the Road* (2000), where, at times, a series of disconnected memories seem to be almost randomly strung together. Like Joyce (2000), Maher has a particular purpose in writing, even if that intention is as fluid as the desire to celebrate Traveller storytelling and culture. Unlike Joyce's (2000) and a number of other more recent Traveller autobiographies (e.g. Cawley, 2004; Dunne, 2004) that have been mediated through a tape recorder or an interview process, Maher wrote his memoir himself.

Born in 1932, the eldest child of an unhappy Traveller "match", young Seán expresses the desire to receive a formal education and cherishes hopes of becoming a priest, two aspirations which encounter suspicion, incomprehension or hostility on the part of some other Travellers, his father, in particular. His dream of receiving an education proves elusive until, he runs away from his family at the age of twelve. Malnutrition and exposure leave him deathly ill with pneumonia and it is while he is in hospital that a concerned social worker intervenes on his behalf so that he can be sent to school rather than returning to live with his parents. He then receives four years of formal education at which, by his own accounts, he excels, at least partly because he is highly motivated. In Maher's opinion, his education is a source of difference that makes him a partial outsider to his own community. This in-between status may account for the uncertainty and ambivalence that is the characteristic tone of his memoir. Maher exhibits mixed feelings towards aspects of "traditional" Traveller culture in much the same way that Azade Seyhan (cited in Lanters) describes the immigrant experience: – as "'a conversation between opposing voices or … conflicting self-perceptions of ethnic groups … [T]he narrator is caught in an ambiguous … discourse of … conflicting loyalties or preferences'" (Seyhan cited in Lanters 2005, 38). Although Travellers are indigenous to Ireland and are not immigrants, they, too, have to negotiate between two differing cultures. In Maher's case, these "conflicting loyalties" may also be of a personal nature. While his style is anecdotal, with much space given over to traditional storytelling, a clear sense of his own family dynamic is revealed, including the psychological and emotional pain caused by the verbal abuse and beatings Seán suffered from his father.

The *Road to God Knows Where* (1998) exhibits many of the characteristics of the "split" self that Gilmore (1994) typifies as an element of the "masculinist" text. Maher (1998) actively interprets his past, a self-reflexivity that requires the writing "I" to objectify the "I" of the past. With the benefit of the experience and understanding gained over subsequent years, the writing "I" can offer an "objective" view of events, one which is almost as good as an outsider's. According to Gilmore (1994), this splitting technique which functions as "a dialogue that takes a split self as speaker / knower" (1994, 46), is similar to the one employed by Saint Augustine whose *Confessions* has become a template for modern autobiography. In Maher's (1998) text, this psychological "splitting" plays out through his cast of characters. Maher assigns ownership of each story he recounts to specific "characters", usually allowing them to relate their stories as a first-person narrative. Occasionally the pattern differs and he relates the story on their behalf, but he never does this without crediting the originator of the story beforehand. A similar deference towards the teller of the tale, as exhibited in other storytelling societies, suggests that some stories "belong" to certain individuals. This "belonging" or ownership is not something which is exhibited in the legalistic sense – i.e. in which an author owns a copyright - but in the more reverential sense whereby the "story" is part of that person's life and cannot (out of respect) be borrowed by another without permission. The assignment of a particular story to a certain individual storyteller also suggests that both the teller and the tale become associated with a specific time or place.

As with Joyce (2000), Maher's characters propose orality as a legitimate form of knowledge, although the multivocality of his text permits opposing views that simultaneously problematize such an assertion. His partial fictionalizing of characters gives the writer the freedom to explore diverse views without having to identify with a particular viewpoint or be associated with it, – i.e. without having to take an "authoritative" position. His strategy suggests that these "characters", who often bear nicknames as opposed to real (actual) names, are as much personas as "real" people. Appearing and disappearing through all of these characters and their stories and dialogues, Maher creates that same "de-centred" self which parallels postmodern notions of subjectivity. In this way, Maher diverges from the aforementioned Augustinian autobiographical template that validates the memoirist's self. Maher's narrative incorporating characters within the framework of a memoir creates a forum for contrasting voices to emerge; a framework which allows Seán to recede as an individual into the cultural milieu as an observer. As the chief-storyteller and writer, however, Maher is still in a position to manipulate the narrative as appropriate to his needs.

Maher does not write with any obvious political agenda but his emphasis on representations of various aspects of Traveller tradition and culture ensures the preservation of traditional stories and songs that might otherwise have been lost. Since the era Maher writes about - his memoir ends sometime in the 1950s — Traveller culture has experienced similar types of change and assimilationist pressures that have affected many other indigenous minority cultures throughout the world. Committing oral storytelling to print tends to reify what is essentially a "one-off" and dynamic performance that is responsive to a particular audience and locale. That Maher takes pains to establish the storytelling experience in a specific setting and to place the story in the mouth of a particular raconteur offers a partial solution to this difficulty of transcribing what is essentially an oral performance into writing. Despite this intervention on Maher's part, an onus remains on the reader to fill in the gaps between the "presentness" and the performativity of the storytelling act, thereby obviating an undue reification of a written text that is representative of dynamic recitation. Predictions made by a number of Maher's characters concerning the assimilation and cultural disappearance of Travellers as a people – or, at least, their traditional nomadic lifestyle – encounters the paradox inherent in Maher's memoir. The very act of writing, including the intention of preserving traditions which the narrator views as imperilled, means that Maher's own written record tends to disprove the very predictions of cultural annihilation that his characters voice within the text.

Historical Narrative and the Conception of Time

The unique nature of Joyce and Maher's text raises a number of important questions concerning the disjunction between the oral and literary worlds. Subtle yet fundamental differences between the oral and literary worldviews, for example, account for the difficulty - at certain junctures - for Anna Farmar (as editor) to fashion some of Joyce's loosely-connected anecdotes into the coherence of a purely realistic text. The modern Western mind thinks of time as "linear, sequential, and unidirectional, like an arrow" (Suzuki and Knudtson 1992, 177). The evident struggle to achieve narrative cohesion in *My Life on the Road* is, in part, due to a particular view of time as evidenced in oral cultures, one where there is much less emphasis on linearity. More important, and thus more evident in the writings of Maher and Joyce is the circularity of the various annual life cycles. This partially accounts for the absence of a definitive narrative trajectory and is another way whereby both Maher and Joyce depart from previous autobiographical templates. Maher's chapters tend to be episodic and are normally associated with the people with whom he is having a dialogue at this particular point in his life. Joyce's anecdotes are recounted in a direct style that creates a very real sense of a present-time orientation, one which only rarely portends future developments. Although Farmar has rearranged Joyce's spoken anecdotes chronologically in *My Life on the Road*, it is as if Joyce does not imagine her life in terms of a (definitive) linear progression. Farmar's arrangement of the text, including the last chapter, represents a type of conclusion or resolution to the narrative whereby Joyce hopes for improved conditions for Travellers. In a sense, Joyce's anecdotes attest to an almost-predictable regularity in the cycle of forced evictions, poor housing and consequent ill-health. This daily struggle for survival may in part account for the "intense present-time orientation" (Ní Shúinéar 1994, 60) many theorists[13] have identified as intrinsic to nomadic cultures. Ong (1967, 1991) finds the same propensity in oral cultures; an ongoing necessity to expunge information that is no longer useful. (Of course, memory works this way for all people. On a daily basis, every one tends to remember what they consider to be important and to slough off the rest.) Contradicting the "present-time" generalization, oral cultures such as the Hebrew tribes were obsessed with genealogies as recorded in the Pentateuch (see Numbers). This meticulous recording of a primeval past implies not only a notion of time that assumes a historical teleology, but also indicates generational continuity as a shaper of present-day identity evident in other societies like Travellers' where the extended family forms the basis of community.

Travellers, of course, like everyone else also think about the future. Why otherwise would Maher have made such great efforts to become educated? Why would Joyce have worked assiduously to improve present conditions for Travellers – was she not also thinking of her children and grandchildren? Bridget Gaffey (1992), one of the contributors to a collection of short autobiographical compositions and poems, *Moving Stories: Traveller Women Write*, is clearly thinking of the future when she writes in the preface to this volume, "Some women in the group have written about how things used to be because these days are now completely different for the Travelling people … those times are gone, never to return. We want to let the next generation know how it used to be" (1992, 8).

When making theoretical generalizations, especially about people who have been disadvantaged by marginalization, the scholar must consider

---

[13] Lanters (2005) quotes Noonan's assertion that "the Traveller community 'is very much present-time oriented'" (Noonan cited by Lanters 2005, 27). Ironically, such declarations come at a period of advanced consumerism that, as Terry Eagleton has remarked, encourage the subject "to live provisionally" (Eagleton 1991, 198).

whether the apparent truth contained in the observation is inherent, or if certain behaviours relate to particular life conditions and contexts. Before one deems people intrinsically "present-minded", one would have to enquire into those external conditions that keep life short and harsh[14]. "Present-time" inclinations are partly a consequence of orality, and a concession to the limited memory of the human brain (although important memories are preserved and transmitted through storytelling); they can also function as a defensive mechanism which enables the human psyche to face an uncertain future in a more hopeful frame of mind.

Although Maher's memoir refrains from the linearity usually associated with a realist narrative, his apocalyptic tone reflects the very essence of Western concepts of time as derived from the Biblical model where world history begins with the Creation and ends with the Apocalypse. Nonetheless, in view of Maher's otherwise episodic narrative, this concept of the end of time[15] may be indicative of the influence of his education. To this day, it is a facet of societies where people depend on seasonal and harvest variations – e.g. hunter-fisher and small-scale agrarian and nomadic societies – that time tends to be conceived as a cyclical pattern – or as it is lived. This cyclical view of time contradicts a typical Enlightenment discourse that conceives of human history as a linear progression, a history that is always moving forward in accordance with "our … notions of 'progress'" (Suzuki and Knudtson 1992, 177) that still pervade modern-day Western discourse. Generally, the modern concept of time permits a view of history that reduces a complex pattern of social, cultural, technological, economic and environmental interactions to be represented as a narrative of "events" that contain "an underlying, meaningful, and rational structure" (Flax 1990, 31). Historiography, Michel de Certeau (1988) posits, an integral element in this modern discourse, is essentially "history making" since in all realist narratives, historians exercise a process of selection based on a series of pre-existing paradigms so that "[t]hey seem to tell of facts while, in effect, they express *meanings* [my emphasis] which moreover refer what is *noted* (what historians hold to be relevant) to a conception of whatever is *notable*" (de

---

[14] Having reached her mid-sixties, Nan Joyce represents just three per cent of the Traveller population over sixty-five as compared to eleven per cent of the general population ("Traveller Community" 2005, 2). This figure is partly attributable to the high birthrate amongst Travellers ("Traveller Community" 2005, 2), but there remains the fact that "Traveller women live on average 12 years less than women in the general population" (Joyce citing a Department of Health and Children Report, *Traveller Health: A National Strategy 2002-2005*, 2002, 1).

[15] Eliade notes that the 'end' always contains a beginning.

Certeau 1988, 42). The conception of time as linear and life as a process which is moving onwards towards a conclusion translates so well to narrative forms that "[Roland] Barthes places it in direct relation with … the realistic novel" (de Certeau 1988, 42). A similar process of meaning-making that occurs in writing "life as narrative" necessitates filling in the gaps, the false starts, the impasses and the inconsistencies, so as to create the illusion of linearity. This process employs memory as forgetting (what is deemed unimportant) and memory as remembering (what is deemed significant) within "interpretive frameworks" (Rakow and Wackwitz 2004, 173), all of which aids the individual (or social group / culture / nation) in constructing a sense of identity. Such omissions are usually passed over in silence, in part because they go unrecognized, as they are unconscious. While interpretive frameworks are socially and culturally informed and in this sense "inherited" (as social construction proponents have minutely explored), the capacity of human activity and imagination to move beyond received wisdom is further explored through some of Nan Joyce's vignettes as outlined in Part I. In both Joyce (2000) and Maher's (1998) work, importance tends to be placed on relations, both in the sense of human relations, as well as relationality as an organizing criterion.

Concepts of time represent only one of the cultural differences that can become problematic if they are not recognized as potential barriers to understanding. The academic reader possesses a culture of literacy that has tended to devalue oral expressions in the past. That these modes of thinking are not polarities, that computer culture (among other technological tools) is today in the process of inventing creative cultural amalgams, suggests that these cultural variations will not always be construed as an impassable chasm. An awareness and sensitivity to difference can help the academic reader – who occupies a relatively privileged position – to approach those knowledge systems that tend to have been discredited in the absence of sufficient literary credentials. This openness to the examination of alternative viewpoints in a sensitive manner is an attitude many feminist historians have labelled "'epistemic humility'" (cited by Ruth Roach Pierson 1991, 94).

Part I. Challenging Hegemony: The Problem Of Representation

Since "representations" and epistemologies of experience have been both problematized and (sometimes) discredited, and given that these are the languages used by less privileged speakers / writers, Part I of this volume will focus on questions pertaining to representation. Dyer (1993) argues that representations concern the manner in which others view a particular group, in addition to how a group views itself (Dyer 1993, 1), and that these viewpoints also symbolize various power relations. Joyce (2000) and other Travellers are fully aware of the types of stereotypes that circulate among the general population about Travellers (see Hayes, 2000). She challenges negative stereotypes, often in a direct "head-on" fashion, a blunt approach that reflects the "deep agonistic roots" (Ong 1991, 111) of oratory. This agonistic style may appear somewhat discomfiting to the reader who is more attuned to the subtleties of "erudite" or more sophisticated argumentation. José Lanters (2005) has noted for us that these refutations can, on occasion, seem to be somewhat "defensive" in nature, although it is not clear what alternative strategies would be as effective in such a situation.

While Joyce's tactics may not always succeed, challenging domination remains an essential part of the struggle for Travellers who wish to assert the cultural legitimacy of their community. As Shari Stone-Mediatore (2003) notes:

> [T]he prejudices that prevail in a society are those that are circulated by dominant social groups and that rationalize dominant social institutions. No one escapes the influence of such ruling beliefs; however, dominant social groups benefit from ruling beliefs while the more marginalized groups endure the contradictions of those beliefs and the institutions they rationalize in resulting practical conditions in their lives. (2003, 89)

For Joyce, the difficulty remains that she has to employ the vocabularies of a hegemonic culture while attempting to legitimize positions that may sometimes stand outside the parameters of "majority" society norms. Stone-Mediatore (2003) has explored this quandary further by drawing in Gadamer's[16] (1900-2002) findings regarding those values which are embedded in the very language we speak:

> When the more socially powerful groups have greater control over the institutions that produce and distribute knowledge, those groups can widely disseminate their views and present their views as if they were universal truths. Such socially produced "common sense" beliefs inform academic and popular discourses and, consequently, affect the whole

---

[16] Hans-Georg Gadamer was a prominent figure in the development of twentieth century hermeneutics. His emphasis both in his thinking and in its application was on a "dialogical" approach (Malpas 2005).

> community's way of thinking. Such beliefs thus tend to remain unnoticed and untested. (2003, 78)

Despite the hurdles, Joyce (2000) goes to great lengths so as to "reconfigure" the terms of her discourse so that it will be as accessible as possible to any type of reader.

Joyce trusts that her life story can act as a catalyst for political change. It is important to pay close attention to the approaches she employs to do just that. In the process, it may be possible to go beyond the discourse (including direct rebuttals) that Lanters identifies as "defensive" and explore the alternative discursive strategies employed by Joyce. Joyce's appropriation of familiar images, for example, is one alternative strategy whereby she cleverly inverts the usual connotations associated with certain images, problematizing their underlying assumptions. The alternative points of view which Traveller writers highlight are crucial to creating a "balance" within a homogeneous society since they serve to challenge and destabilize dominant beliefs and evoke a response, a debate and (on occasion), a dialogue.

Part II. Alternative History: Writing Travellers into the Nation's Discourse

Having examined various ways that Joyce challenges prejudicial attitudes, we now move onto an examination of Joyce (2000) and Maher's (1998) creative rewriting of Irish national discourse. So that Travellers have a "place" within the national discourse, Joyce's inclusion of MacColl's poem / song, "The Moving-on Song", intertwined within the autobiographical text that is *My Life on the Road*, represents both the quest for Traveller inclusion (i.e., belonging) and the physical struggle for actual living space in an environment encompassing forced evictions and systemic persecution. The poem's didacticism parallels the poetic patterns and usages of the medieval era where the intimate connections between poetry and public life represent the oral and agonistic traditions. Metaphorical approaches encompassing history as story-making include Traveller versions of apocryphal myths which offer positive models that usurp the negative constructs applied to Travellers by others. These counter-narratives (see O hAodha 2004) re-inscribe Travellers into the history of the Irish nation-state, a narrative from which they have been effaced. By the process of speaking history, Travellers make claims for orality as a legitimate form of knowledge and thereby destabilize the hegemonic mythmaking of (predominantly) literate societies that valorizes the written word above all else. By directly addressing an historical omission, by the presentation of imaginative counter-narratives, Joyce and Maher reappropriate national mythologies so as to include Travellers in a more positive, participatory role in the formation of the new Irish nation-state. Maher's characters relate inspiring stories of struggle similar in their heroism to the narratives promulgated by sectors of the Anglo-Irish Literary Revival narratives, which posited a glorious legendary Irish past as a counterpoint to English domination. Maher's retelling of these myths from a Traveller perspective usurps commonly-held assumptions with respect to "who gets to frame and to tell the story — whose voices are prominent and whose are marginalized" (Cruikshank 2005, 2). By underlining both the importance of Traveller participation within the historical development of the modern Irish nation-state and its historical constructions, Joyce and Maher reinforce their claim and the claims of the minority they "represent" to full-citizenship and full participation in the bounty of the state.

Part III. Rewriting the Modern: Countering "Anglo-Saxon Empiricism"

Part III investigates various modes of narration used by Joyce and Maher, all of which reveal worldviews that are contrary to the rational materialism which typifies modernity. The section opens with a discussion of the first of two "miracle" stories recounted by Maher's mother, i.e., the miracle at Colaney Well. Reverence for holy places in Ireland is a tradition that is centuries-old and pilgrimages to these sites were once a common feature of Irish life, particularly amongst the rural population. Luke Gibbons (1996) argues that Irish expressions of piety that derived from pre-Christian traditions and popular belief were brought under the centralizing control of the Roman Church in the post-Famine (1845-9) era. Angela Bourke (1995, 1996) corroborates this view and interweaves this "centralizing" tendency with the linguistic and cultural reactions in the post-Famine trauma, including the backlash by the growing Irish middle-class against all that was traditionally Irish – including orality and the Irish language.

The apocalyptic tendency evident in the stories Maher recounts (as related by his mother) offers a different strategy in an effort to cope with the effects of large-scale psychic trauma. It is difficult for the *secular* mind to imagine the kind of life circumstances that can envision the annihilation of one's people within religious paradigms of sin and redemption and yet be comforted, as Maher's mother seems to be in relating St. Kevin's dire predictions for Travellers. Apocalyptic forecasts as a consequence of trauma must be explored. The dollman's anti-modernism provides a background of struggle that helps to contextualize these dire predictions. The views expressed by Maher's characters highlight the contradictions of "progress"; perspectives that tend to remain ignored in more official economic analyses where development tends to be represented as having only positive results.

Joyce strongly disputes the kind of fatalism evident in Maher. Her ability to question and to depart from widely-held social conventions is expressed through her activism. In spite of editor Anna Farmar's best efforts to fashion a narrative, anecdotes that attribute supernatural significance to events work to disrupt conventional realist expectations, this despite the fact that Joyce relates these occurrences as if they were a natural part of everyday life. Her blending of the mystical and mysterious into ordinary life reinstils a sense of oneness with her world, one which characterizes a worldview that Ong attributes to orality. Because sound is a "unifying sense" (Ong 1991, 72), oral cultures and those still deeply influenced by oral traditions interpret the world as a cosmos, a universe filled with meaning, a world that mirrors a greater reality. Joyce's "mystical" experiences suggest the immanence of God, an attitude that Noel Dermot O'Donoghue (1989, 2001) identifies as typical of "Celtic" Christianity, but which Mircea Eliade (1959) finds generally present throughout European rural cultures. In contrast, the characteristic modern "culture of intense inwardness" (Sass 1997, 205) that typifies the isolated Cartesian self leads to a sense of separation from the world. The distancing mechanism that Ong ascribes to an emphasis on the visual that language as print has encouraged, allows for the objectivity of scientific enquiry. This approach promulgates a view of the world as a purely material entity encompassing mechanistic phenomena to be investigated. The worldviews evident in Traveller writing act as a counterbalance to the rationalist materialism still predominant within much Western thinking and institutional life generally.

Attitudes expressing reverence for the natural world will next be examined in Joyce's poem "The Beauty I Can See" (1994). Though not appearing in her autobiography, the poem is of interest because of the ways that Joyce takes a traditional genre, the Irish nature poem and explores the Irish landscape as a metonym[17] for patriotic nationalism. At the same time, she portrays the Traveller presence as integral to this

[17] Even though considered a literary device, this term is more applicable here. (See Lanham 1991, 101).

landscape. A comparable synthesis of Travellers and landscape appears at an early stage of her autobiography (2000) where a childhood memory situates Travellers within the historical Irish landscape through the action that is the narration of history. Maher's memoir (1998) concludes with an exultation of nature, the natural world which mitigates the often-grim circumstances and tone evoked in the preceding pages. This narrative strategy is one which permits a more expansive approach, one which offers hope while at the same time circumventing the narrative obligation that is a dénouement.

Mircea Eliade (1959) has identified the almost mystical experience that nature can generate – an experience which is strongly evident in both Joyce (2000) and Maher (1998). Eliade (1959) links this experience with the intimate relationship which rural people throughout Europe share with nature and which he ascribes to an amalgam of both Christian and pre-Christian belief (1959, 164). In the case of Ireland, these pre-Christian customs can be traced to the cultural underlay of ancient mythologies and druidic practices that were once held as common belief. Rather than interpret this responsiveness to the natural world as an anachronism, a worldview which allows for such close interaction with non-human life reflects contemporary concerns for the environment (e.g. the global warming issue), particularly for people who believe that a radical change in philosophy is vital so as to eliminate environmentally-destructive practices. Present-day environmentalists frequently argue that the ethical myopia of the scientific paradigm permits the thinking that will ultimately lead to environmental destruction. It is no surprise, therefore, that some environmentalists, David Suzuki (1992, 1997), for example, are turning to the traditions of oral cultures in order to find ways to bridge these looming ethical crises. It is only by narrowing the conceptual separation that exists between human beings and the natural world – many environmentalists argue – that the human race may generate an enhanced awareness and respect for the interrelatedness between the human species and its environment, and construct more ethical, and ecologically-sound practices in the process.

This volume examines the ways in which Travellers re-write themselves into the Irish national story through a re-appropriation of established paradigms and the addressing of contemporary issues, which affect their community. They describe the nation and their place within it from perspectives which have not always been given due recognition. When listened to, their points of view can illuminate not only the things that are lost, but also, what is worth keeping for the future. Because they are writing from the periphery of Irish society, their elliptical perspectives capture aspects of the Irish experience from a point of view which permits a very self-reflexive exploration that bolsters their desire for equal citizenship, but also mirrors a range of issues which affect Irish culture as a whole. Stone-Mediatore (2003) suggests that heeding the viewpoints of people marginalized within a democracy strengthens the democratic processes that such a society professes to value. Furthermore, within the specifically Irish context, a deeper look at the history of colonialism suggests that anti-Traveller persecution is, at least in part, a consequence of a buried yet unresolved trauma associated with the colonial legacy.

History and the Postcolonial Legacy

"… the roads was narrower but the land was wider" (Chrissie Ward, 1992)

When one considers all that Irish Travellers and non-Travellers hold in common, a theoretical framework which helps contextualize what may (otherwise) seem an inexplicable historical prejudice is necessary in order to identify the historical and ideological background to the racism outlined in these various Traveller texts. While no one theory can fully explain the complexities that permit long-standing prejudice against a particular minority group, this volume nevertheless explores the historical and philosophical contexts to a greater degree than the psychological perspectives [18]. Jim Mac Laughlin (1995, 1999) finds a relation between anti-Traveller racism and the Enlightenment philosophies that gave birth to the modern European nation-state. Both Judith Okely (1983) and Jane Helleiner (2000) cite historical documents which outline suspicious attitudes and the ensuing persecution of Travelling groups well before the advent of the modern state; the child's nursery rhyme that serves to introduce Nan Joyce's *My Life on the Road* (2000) points to the pervasiveness of this mind-set. Michael Hayes (2006) argues convincingly that racist rhetoric depicting Travellers as an "aberrant" people closely emulates more "generic" English attitudes towards the Irish people as a whole under colonial rule. Having internalized these negative opinions, the non-Traveller Irish population projects their "otherness" onto the Traveller minority in their midst, associating their "trauma", "marginalization",

[18] This volume does not foreground psychological models such as Julia Kristeva's musings on the "abject" or anthropologist Mary Douglas's similar observations about purity and pollution. However, psychological models that examine the dynamics of "othering" anathemetical groups can be usefully applied. Certainly, rhetoric of "pollution" and "purity" are often utilized, even contemporaneously, to justify persecution.

piety, and preference for nomadism as analogous with a colonial history epitomizing a sense of defeat which the majority Irish have not yet come to terms with (see also Ní Shuinéar 1994, 2002). Jim Sheridan's film version (1990) of John B. Keane's play of the same name, *The Field* (1980), will aid us in an identification of some of the colonial residues that lie at the root of "anti-nomadism" in Ireland. The important symbolic role that Travellers occupy in Sheridan's screenplay highlights the "settled" community's anxieties, regarding landlessness as the antithesis to the traditional, rural, patriarchal values the protagonist, small farmer Bull McCabe clings to. Rendering Ireland as a nation haunted by its past, the movie portrays the trauma of the Potato Famine as an unhealed scar on the national psyche. In this context, the disputed field becomes an arena where the Bull continues to wage colonial struggles.

The Discourse of Sedentarism

Robbie McVeigh (1997, 2002) defines "sedentarism" as "'that system of ideas and practices which serves to normalize and reproduce sedentary modes of existence and pathologise and repress nomadic modes of existence'" (1997, 9). Jim Mac Laughlin (1995, 1999) traces anti-nomadism to the same Enlightenment philosophies that also legitimised European colonisation worldwide. Adam Smith[19] (1723-90) hypothesized a view that saw human history as a progression characterized by a number of predictable stages of development whereby nomadism was gradually supplanted by sedentarism (Mac Laughlin 1995, 24). In a similar fashion, John Locke (1632-1704) linked the move to private property as opposed to communal ownership as "the abandonment of 'primitive' lifestyles" (Mac Laughlin 1995, 24). The worldview that no longer linked ownership rights with occupancy but with evidence of "development" was one which permitted the "legal" expropriation of "unused"[20] land from a wide range of nomadic peoples. Societies became hierarchized according to resource utilization, a criterion which:

[19] Smith's book, *The Wealth of Nations* (1776), had a "profound influence on modern economics and concepts of individual freedom" (Chew 2007).

[20] The quotation marks are used to indicate that these definitions were unilateral on the part of the "law makers" and interpreters who also happened to be the European colonizers. In other words, Western "international" law tended to be applied worldwide in all cases where European culture encountered non-European cultures.

> [L]egitimised the domination of nomadic societies in the colonies by white 'settlers' and ... justified the marginalization of nomadic groups including Gypsies, Travellers and the rural poor within Europe, on the grounds that, as propertyless people, they had no right to be included within the political or moral structures of European societies. (Mac Laughlin 1995, 23)

In spite of the principles of egalitarianism that modern liberal democracies espoused, the philosophies that helped formulate these new political systems frequently excluded certain peoples – including nomads – as undesirable citizens.

According to Mac Laughlin (1995, 1999), the devaluing of nomadism is concomitant with the rise of the modern nation-state in the seventeenth and eighteenth centuries and the valorization of "bourgeois nationalist ideas about homeland, property, hygiene and respectability" (Mac Laughlin 1999, 129). Although his argument is a convincing one, his hypothesis does not explain the evidence of earlier persecutions enforced against Travellers and Gypsies in European countries. Okely (1983) is more thorough in tracing the various edicts and pogroms enacted from the time the Roma's arrival in Europe was first alluded to sometime in the 16th century (Okely 1983, 3). The presence of "Gypsies" was first recorded in England in 1505 – around the same time as "tinkers"[21] are first referred to. By 1554, both Travellers and Gypsies (Roma) were being imprisoned or deported in accordance with increasingly repressive anti-nomadic measures enacted under British law. In England at this time, a major shift in economic and agricultural practices was forcing the rural labouring populations from the land and into cities. Such social upheavals were seen as a potential source of instability and ferment across Europe. The authorities (generally aristocracies) in a number of countries sought to control nomadism, and instigated a range of edicts against "vagrants". Helleiner (2000) finds evidence of a similar mistrust of nomadic people as contemporaneous to the Tudor "'re-conquest'" in Ireland (Helleiner 2000, 31), a fact which also indicates the threat which nomadism was considered to pose well before the development of the modern Irish nation-state. Pre-conquest Ireland was a pastoral society with "many itinerant occupational groups" but, as Helleiner (2000) observes, the "mobility of Gaelic society" became associated with "'barbarism'" (Helleiner 2000, 31) in the minds of

[21] "Tinker" was used to designate Travellers by non-Travellers until recent times, but Travellers do not generally refer to themselves as Tinkers. There is still insufficient evidence to determine if these early references to "tinkers" are referring to Irish Travellers, Roma (often referred to as "English Gypsies"), to practitioners of a trade (tinsmiths or "tinkers"), or to other sections of displaced populations (see Michael Hayes, 2006).

the British colonizer. Thus, Helleiner (2000) finds that "English colonial discourse and practice from the second half of the sixteenth century" onwards was generally equated with "the 'civilizing' of the Irish" and with the "suppression of mobility" (Helleiner 2000, 31)[22].

The traditional children's rhyme that opens (i.e., as a chapter heading) Nan Joyce's *My Life on the Road* provides evidence of the longstanding pervasiveness of anti-nomadism. The poem reveals the existence of deep-rooted fearful or suspicious attitudes which perceived the Gypsy presence within Europe's increasingly sedentary society as a threat. Functionally, Marlene Kadar (2005) uses the same poem in her essay on the forgotten Roma Holocaust, "The Devouring: Traces of Roma[23] in the Holocaust: No Tattoo, Sterilized Body, Gypsy Girl," citing these verses from Eric Kincaid's (2001) book of nursery rhymes:

> My mother said I never should
> Play with the gypsies in the wood.
> If I did, she'd surely say
> Naughty wan to disobey[24]. (Joyce 1: 1-4)[25]

This is as much of the poem as appears in *My Life on the Road* (2000), but Kadar (2005) continues with the next four lines of the verse that illustrate all of the terrible things that will happen to the disobedient child – thereby presenting a cautionary tale:

> Your hair shan't curl
> And your shoes shan't shine
> You gypsy girl,
> You shan't be mine. (Kadar 239-40: 5-8)

---

[22] Mobility across national borders continues to be one of the characteristics of Traveller nomadism, as Joyce's story exemplifies. Unlike the vast majority of Travellers who live in the Republic, Nan Joyce grew up in Northern Ireland, but as an adult the Joyce family moved between Ireland, Northern Ireland, Scotland and England. As was common practice amongst the settled Irish, such moves were motivated by job opportunities and often involved seasonal employment.

[23] Although generally referred to as "Roma", this term comprises three major groups (with major sub-groups): the Roma, predominantly settled in Eastern Europe (Kalderash), the Sinti of Western Europe (Manouches and Romanichels) and the Kalé of Spain and Portugal ("Myths" 2006, 2).

[24] The lines are split in *My Life on the Road* (2000) for the sake of spacing and appear in columns as a heading. The wording of the first stanza varies slightly between the two texts.

[25] Poetry, where quoted, will be written as page numbers followed by line numbers.

Lines five and six are not so serious, but the following two lines highlight the much more serious consequences of "misbehaviour" (acting outside the "norm") i.e., rejection (or loss of affection) and a "change" in identity. By merely associating with the "Gypsy" threat, the child threatens to cross the "taboo" boundary and become one himself / herself. The next stanza culminates in a complete loss of the child's "identity" with her abduction, as a consequence of her participation in an emblematic Gypsy activity – music-making – i.e., in this case, playing the tambourine, "In came Sally with a tambourine" (Kadar 240: 12), in addition to economic transactions traditionally associated with "marginal" groups such as the Roma, "I paid ten shillings for a blind white horse" (Kadar 240: 14). Money changing hands conjures the well-known association of the Roma with trading, the stereotype of the Gypsy "fence", but the verse also contains supernatural connotations. The blindness of the horse not only suggests a defect but also hints at sorcery, especially given that the same horse immediately carries the child away: "I was up on his back and was off in a crack, / Sally tell my mother I shall never come back." (Kadar 2005, 240: 15-16). The rhyme not only recalls traditional beliefs associating Roma with magical, (often) malevolent (occult) powers, but also re-affirms the once-popular belief that Roma "stole" (white) children[26]. That this poem is a nursery rhyme can be suggestive of innocence, on the one hand. The fact that nursery rhymes have been "standard bearers" for age-old normalizing "vernacular" and formulaic programming means that the verse is also indicative of the predominance of "anti-nomadism" in the European imagination.

Historically, the response to nomadic populations has ranged from the extremes of extermination to the less radical means of elimination by assimilation. When assimilationist policies have failed, civic authorities have sought to control the movement of communities such as Travellers and thereby contain the perceived threat. Though the persecution of nomadic groups within Europe extends back to the early modern period, at least, the methods of controlling the "problem" have been perfected within the apparatus of the modern nation-state. Foucault's (1979, 1980, 1988, 2003) observations on modern administrative techniques finds that "one of the primary objects of discipline is to fix; it is an anti-nomadic technique" (Foucault 1979, 218). He goes on to say, "That is why discipline fixes; it arrests or regulates movements … it dissipates compact groupings of individuals wandering about the country in unpredictable ways; it

[26] To illustrate the prevalence of the "abduction" trope, such an abduction scene is dramatized in Shirley Temple's 1937 American film, *Heidi*.

establishes calculated distributions" (Foucault 1979, 219). The modern state's need to control aberrant behaviour is a primary motivation for the widely accepted practice of "community-planning" as a form of economic segregation and encourages such policies as the forced evictions that are a recurring aspect of Joyce's autobiography. Sibley (1995) underscores the moral undertones of this policing of boundaries by noting that the degree to which differences are construed as violations correlates with the emphasis on "order, conformity and social homogeneity" (Sibley 1995, 38-9) in a society. As Davis observes, "'the greater the search for conformity, the greater the search for deviance'" (Davis cited in Sibley 1995, 38-9). Such was the case in Ireland according to historian J.J. Lee who argued that the newly independent Republic "desperately" tried to establish unity "on a basis of homogeneity and mass conformity" (Lee cited by McLouglin 1994, 85).

Since early modern times, ethnic mobility has been perceived as a threat by authorities precisely because it epitomizes a lack of control or an unknown societal element. In "Theorising Sedentarism: The Roots of Anti-Nomadism", McVeigh (1997) further elaborates on the tradition that is the suppression of nomadism as a moral imperative. Having "internalised the dominant ideology of sedentarised identity and individual property rights" (1997, 22), the "settled" community feel threatened because the nomadism in their midst "subvert[s] deep-seated beliefs about the normalcy of settlement and wage labour and private property" (1997, 22). Writing five years later, in the introduction to *Racism and Anti-Racism in Ireland* (2002), McVeigh and Lentin focus on the systemization of this persecution and conclude, "The inequality experienced by Travellers can no longer be dismissed as a consequence of nomadism … because sedentary Irish society in general — and the state in Ireland in particular — discriminates against Travellers, routinely, structurally and in a racist manner" (2002, 23). In the same essay, the authors quote Noonan's analysis confirming the systemic nature of this racism: "Being a Traveller[27] … involves low life expectancy, high infant mortality and morbidity, low educational achievement, appalling living conditions and differential access to a range of state services" (Noonan cited in McVeigh and Lentin 2002, 23).

Colonialism contextualizes the specific circumstances of anti-nomadism in Ireland and is an issue which necessitates analysis prior to focusing on the principle texts discussed here. In "Othering the Irish (Travellers)" Ní Shúinéar (2002) links racist discourses with Ireland's

[27] Parallel circumstances affect the First Nations of Canada.

colonial legacy. Just as Irish men were once depicted as apes abusing and exploiting the hapless, downtrodden Irish woman, Traveller men are also sometimes depicted as lazy, feckless, violent and increasingly "redundant", i.e., "'not useful as family builders'",[28] unable to economically sustain their families, "in other words … write-offs" (2002, 188). Familiar stereotypes continue to depict Travellers as dirty, uneducated, shiftless tax and social welfare cheats; and more prone to violence, crime and alcoholism by nature. Ní Shúinéar (2002) argues convincingly that the settled Irish, rather than confronting the trauma inflicted on the collective psyche by centuries of colonial occupation, have deflected their own internalized self-loathing onto Travellers instead. Certainly, the stereotypes ascribed to Travellers by many in Ireland echo those once directed against the Irish by the English, a rhetoric that was used for centuries to justify colonial occupation as a "civilizing" influence. Ní Shúinéar notes the consistencies in reductionist imagery as was once employed by the English colonial regime when she writes, "From the very beginning … backwardness, nomadism and beggary are portrayed as general Irish characteristics, compounded by superstition (later Popery), anarchy, and a penchant for violence" (2002, 179).

While Mac Laughlin (1995, 1999) fails to extend the history of persecution back to the pre-modern era, he correctly notes the emergence of "Social Darwinism" (1999, 129) in the second half of the nineteenth century, a body of theory which provided the framework for a more racialized nationalist discourse that alleged a scientific basis. To illustrate the increased racialism of British colonial rhetoric as fashionable subsequent to Charles Darwin's *Origin of the Species* (1849), Ní Shúinéar (2002) cites well-known British historian Charles Kingsley. In this quote from a letter Kingsley wrote while visiting Ireland in 1860 (a few years after the Famine had devastated rural communities), the Irish are both racialized and portrayed as animals: "'I am haunted by the human chimpanzees I saw along that hundred miles of horrible country,'" he writes. "'To see white chimpanzees is dreadful; if they were black, one would not feel it so much, but their skins, except where tanned by exposure, are as white as ours'" (Kingsley cited in Ní Shúinéar 2002, 180). Political cartoons published in the English, American and Canadian newspapers of the day regularly depicted simian characters, a visual code immediately recognizable to the reader as representing the Irish male[29] (Ní

[28] Here, Ní Shúinéar cites a newsletter published by the Association of Teachers of Travelling People (1979).

[29] Irish women were most often represented by "Hibernia", a virtuous but harried female.

Shúinéar 2002, 181). Similar depictions sometimes occur in the non-Traveller rhetoric concerning Travellers – whether in the more polite bureaucratic language which shapes public policy or in the vitriolic fulminations of the popular media. In the *Sunday Independent* (28 Jan 1996), journalist Mary Ellen Synon employs the type of animal imagery the English once used to describe the Irish when she writes that Traveller culture "is a life of appetite ungoverned by intellect … a life worse than the life of beasts, for beasts at least are guided by some wholesome instinct" ("Travellers in Ireland" 2005, 5). She implies the existence of some sort of innate criminality within the Traveller community. "This tinker 'culture' … is a morass. And one of the surprising things about it is that not every individual bred in this swamp turns out bad. Some individuals among the tinkers find the will not to become evil" ("Travellers in Ireland" 2005, 5). These examples bolster Dyer's (1993) observation that mainstream representations of cultural minorities can be used to oppress, control and exclude, and then to justify these practices.

Examining non-Traveller writing about Travellers highlights some of the ways in which nomads are imagined. The Traveller becomes the "outsider" who is within, a symbol of the perpetual "Other". This example is then repeatedly recruited as representing freedom from social convention, or as a criminal and subversive element, a contaminant within the body of the nation and one which undermines "decent" values. Jim Sheridan's (1990) film version of John B. Keane's play, *The Field*, offers an enhanced characterization of the unsettling "tinker" figure **as** sketched in Keane's original play. In both the theatrical and cinematic versions of *The Field*, the "tinkers", as they are referred to, represent a very real threat to traditional, land-based patriarchy. Sheridan's film version of *The Field* serves as a particularly useful illustration of the types of prejudices that circumvent the figure of the Traveller in latter-day Ireland.

The Legacy of Colonialism: *The Field*

Discriminatory British policies made land a particularly contentious issue throughout Irish history. Who owned the land and who controlled it were crucial issues in an agrarian society such as Ireland's since it (generally) meant the difference between survival and starvation. After the Flight of the Earls in 1607, the year when the remainder of the Irish aristocracy fled to the European continent, the Plantation of Ulster began (Morgan 2007). This British colonial policy confiscated land from

Catholic farmers[30] and gave it to English and Scottish Protestant "Planters" (settlers) who could be counted on as loyal to the British Crown ("Plantation of Ulster"). The Penal Laws, a series of laws passed in the 1690s forbade, among other measures, Irish Catholics from owning land ("Background"). Finally, the Great Famine, 1845-49[31], a catastrophe on a massive scale, changed the demographics of Ireland in a very dramatic way. About one million people were displaced through mass emigration while an estimated one million people died from disease and starvation[32]. Tenant farmers were evicted from their plantations because they were unable to fulfill their fiscal obligations to landlords[33], a fact that would ultimately impact on post-independence Irish government policies in the adoption and implementation of assimilationist policies towards Travellers that were formulated as "re-settlement" policies.

Sheridan's (1990) interpretation of Keane's (1965) play, *The Field,* foregrounds colonialism as a trauma which still resonates strongly in the Irish psyche and in the daily struggle for existence. Protagonist Bull McCabe (played by Richard Harris) has an obsessive desire to own one small field – as representing the legacy of "material" starvation that is the legacy of colonialism. Subsequent to the Famine, this psychic trauma linked self-preservation with land ownership. Small cottiers disappeared; the remaining farmers had more land than they had previously but no longer subdivided their land among their children to the same extent as had once been the practice. The Bull represents the patriarchal values and patrimony of a rural Ireland, that is, even then, in its death-throes.

The action begins when the Widow (played by Frances Tomelty) announces in the local pub that she is putting up one of her fields for auction, a field that has been leased and improved over many years by the McCabe's. The film conveys that this is a "man's world" in many ways. Suspicious male eyes follow the Widow's progress through the centre of

---

[30] Those banished from their lands were forced to live a marginal subsistence on boggy and mountainous land. The "attempt to replace one entire community with another" proved so successful that by 1703 only 5% of Ulster land remained in Catholic hands ("Background").

[31] The first potato crop failed in 1845, and again in 1846. 1847 did not see a catastrophic failure, but yields were very low. There was "a relapse in 1848 and 1849" (Johnston), but the devastating effects of the Famine in the countryside lasted well beyond this date.

[32] Thus, from 1841 to 1851 the population dropped from 8.2 million to 6.5 million (Bloy 2002).

[33] Historian Peter Gray (1995) writes, "between 1849 and 1854 … about a quarter of a million people were permanently evicted from their homes" (1995, 68).

town and into Flanagan's Pub, the exclusive haven of men at that hour of the day. Flanagan reminds the Widow that he cannot serve her alcohol at that hour, but she tells him that she has come to announce the sale by auction of her field. When one of the men asks, "McCabe's field?"[34], the widow corrects him, "He rents it", to which another male voice responds, "It was bare rock when he got it". By time-honoured consensus then, the field belongs to McCabe in all but legal title. According to custom, and in deference to the McCabes' toil that has improved the productivity of this tract of land, the Widow should first offer to sell the land to the Bull at a negotiated price, taking into account the rent he has already paid her. She bypasses this protocol, however, asserting, "I need the best price I can get." By doing this, the Widow affronts an established code of behaviour, an understanding between men, instead as an outsider to the community, choosing to look out for her own security first. Her position as an "outsider" is made abundantly clear in the auction scene when the townspeople jeer at her, "Go back to where you came from!" When the Bull hears of this imminent sale, he drives into town to defend his customary rights to the land. In the pub, he points out that no one from Carraighthomond would dare to make a bid on "his" land and when Flanagan mentions the possibility of "outsiders" at the auction, the Bull launches into a stirring speech that calls up the crimes of British imperialism. In one of the most powerful scenes of the film[35], the Bull recites the hardships endured under British colonialism to a spellbound crowd of locals. The vehemence of his speech underlines the indelible trauma left by the Famine, a trauma that remains raw in the Irish communal memory.

The Bull:

> Outsiders? Are these the same outsiders who took the corn from our mouths when the potatoes were rotting in the ditches? Are these the same outsiders who took the meat from the tables when we lay in the ditches with the grass juice running green from our mouths? Are these the same outsiders who drove us to the coffin ships and scattered us to the four corners of the world? Are these the same outsiders who watched as our valley went silent except for the cries of the last starving child?

At the end of this passionate oration, the publican calmly replies, "The English are gone Bull". Richard Harris's delivery lays just the right degree of forcefulness on Bull's final tirade, "*Gone* because I drove them out. Me and my kind. *Gone* but not forgotten Flanagan. No outsider will bid for my

---

[34] Most quotations are taken directly from the film except where stated otherwise.
[35] This speech does not appear in the original play.

field"[36]. Bull's strong emotional connection to the land derives from a palpable remembrance of the horror and helplessness the Famine's victims felt against the injustice that valued conservative economic models more than simple human compassion. The way of life that the Bull defends – unto the death – is problematized by apparent irresolvable inconsistencies as evident within his own personality or character. He is a brutal, ruthless and driven man, but his obsessions seem to be so intimately interested with the question of land that his "malady" takes on ancestral dimensions — as a consequence of a harsh colonial regime. And yet, as for all his violence and coarseness, there is still a fierce and tormented dignity that he expresses in his ceaseless labour, his obstinate self-sufficiency and (sometimes) chivalrous behaviour as relating to the Widow[37] (i.e., the "weaker" sex)[38]. Whether because of Sheridan's direction or Harris's interpretation[39], this nobility on the part of the Bull elicits a grudging respect for his principled doggedness, even if one rejects the narrow single-mindedness that characterises his values.

While the Widow is still considered an "outsider" to the community after an indeterminate number of years, the Bull carries great influence over the community and conspires with his friends to "rig" the auction so that he can take legal title of the land which he feels is rightfully his. His scheme is stymied by the arrival of a rich outsider intent on bidding for this same field. In both the theatrical and cinematic versions, this outsider is a returned émigré[40]. In Sheridan, the émigré represents the archetypal "returned Yank" (played by Tom Berenger) – bringing with him the taint of "American" economic imperialism. The American personifies "success" achieved as a consequence of emigration[41], a privileged individual who meets with varying degrees of resentment or collaboration on the part of the locals. The American also epitomizes modernization, a motif that is also a recurring theme in the work of Maher (1998). The American is not content to admire the view, but is also intent on innovation and change. Not only does he come to buy the local land with his emigrant money but also plans to make a quarry on the field and harness the waterfall for hydroelectric power so as to run his cement

[36] The italics represent Harris's intonation.
[37] In the play, the Bull also bullies the women.
[38] Interestingly, this "chivalry" does not extend to the "tinker's daughter".
[39] Whereas in the film the Bull is portrayed as alternately instigating and restraining his son's violent acts, in the play he not only incites Tadgh to violence but also is also more brutal.
[40] In Keane, the émigré returns from England.
[41] A similar function is filled by the anglicized William Dee in Keane.

factory — i.e., he literally wants to pave over the ancestral "paradise". Intent on scaring off the American threat, and with an alibi as agreed upon by the other pub patrons, the Bull incites his son, Tadgh (played by Sean Bean) who appears to be suffering from some form of intellectual disability, into giving the "Yank" a sound beating. Unfortunately, the American dies. Father and son hide all evidence of their crime, dumping the body into the sea. A conspiracy of silence falls on the town that after three weeks, the law is still powerless to sway.

While they only merit a passing mention in Keane, Travellers play a prominent, albeit negative role in Sheridan. The Travellers, who appear to be camped very close to the centre of the town for most of the scenes, are ragged, and aggressive and pronounce stereotypical lines such as, "Got any milk for the babby?" If Sheridan is using such stereotypes ironically, this is not very evident. Instead, he appears to provide people over a certain age with a shorthand sketch, a "stage Irishman" caricature that by virtue of its instant recognizability – "tells" an Irish audience – "these are Travellers". The Traveller patriarch has the negative attributes of drinking heavily, is argumentative, and loudly demands "blood money" from the McCabes for the donkey that Tadgh killed for trespassing in their field[42]. In another brief scene, the tinker's daughter (played by Jenny Conroy) – a character who remains nameless[43] – pulls a cart on which her inebriated father lies, unconscious, as if she were a beast of burden.

The tinker's daughter, a red-haired temptress, fills the Traveller / Gypsy stereotype of the sexually-provocative, barely-attainable siren; her rolling eyes, her lolling head, her long tongue licks her lips as she meets Tadgh's eyes with her bold gaze. One Irish film scholar, Cheryl Temple Herr (2002) describes her as "glamorous" (2002, 45), which is apt if what Herr means by glamorous is the one-dimensional, exoticized caricature of Travellers and Roma in non-Traveller artistic and visual representations, a caricature which has a very old history (see Cottaar et al. (1998); Hancock, The Roma: Myth and Reality, Patrin Web Journal (1999); Hayes (2007) etc). Herr's (2002) reference to the emigration "wake" dance scene as "gothic primitivism" would seem to be a more appropriate description of the tinker girl's demeanour, given the primeval "archetype" the tinker girl appears to represent in this scene. At the dance, the Bull is trying to match Tadgh with a suitable dancing partner, a local farmer's daughter who stands to inherit some land. Tadgh is distracted by the "outsider" that is the tinker's daughter, however. Her disruptive presence destabilizes Bull's

[42] Sheridan's movie opens with father and son dumping the donkey's carcass in the sea.

[43] Neither the Widow nor the tinker's daughter are given names in the movie.

carefully-planned maneuvers. Like the American, she is an "outsider" to communal traditions, and a figure who appears to view traditions in which she herself has no stake, as both illogical and stultifying. Moving from one man to the next on the perimeter of the dance floor, the tinker girl taunts the "virility" of the male dancers, in turn: "You're all afraid of me, the tinker's daughter. Will you dance with me? Will you dance with me? You're afraid that if you touch me, you'll lose the soil under your feet and end up sleeping under the stars." Her mockery runs much deeper than a simple taunt. It goes to the core of the men's most cherished beliefs and prejudices (as fostered within their community). Just when Tadgh seems about to accept the Traveller girl's offer, the Bull takes her as his dance partner instead.

After the murder of the American, Tadgh overhears his parents discuss his older brother's suicide, a "shameful" taboo subject which has led to a coldness within his parent's marriage. The circumstances of his brother's death are a revelation to Tadgh since his parents rarely spoke to one another and have never spoken of his dead brother. Overwhelmed by the shocking revelation, he has now become privy to, Tadgh flees his father's home in the dead of night. His flight represents a symbolic break from his father's domination, a rite of passage; one which culminates with Tadgh's arrival at the Traveller's campfire where the "tinker girl" is sitting all alone. The girl's siblings, her parents and all of the other members of the Traveller extended family, as seen earlier, have seemingly disappeared and the Traveller girl functions as a symbol of freedom, an emissary of social and sexual liberation, one which disrupts the conservative morals imposed by community and Church.

The figure of the Traveller functions in this scene in much the same fashion as the tinker woman in J.M. Synge's comedy, *The Tinker's Wedding*, first staged in London in 1909, a play where a romanticized "outsider" figure, a "generic" Traveller character, serves as a projection for the unfulfilled desires of a society which Synge, and his fellow "Revival" writers considered overly-Catholic and stultifying. Synge's "tinkers" exemplify Michael Hayes's (2006) observation that historically, representations of Travellers by non-Traveller Irish writers have tended to mirror the "colonial 'stage Irishman'", a stock character who plays the part of "the happy-go-lucky vagrant, the criminal, the drunk, the storyteller and the outcast" (2006, 243-4).

When Sarah Casey decides that she and her common-law husband Michael Byrne must be married by the Church, her mother-in-law, Mary Byrne, who is opposed to the prospect of an officially-sanctioned marriage as a moral obligation, inadvertently sabotages their plans by using part of the pre-agreed payment due to the priest to buy herself alcohol. After the priest refuses to marry the Traveller couple, an argument ensues, one which escalates until – worried that the priest will call the "peelers" (i.e., the police) down on them – Michael Byrne gags the priest and ties a sack over his head. The three Travellers convince the priest to take an oath of silence and then release him from the sack. The priest pronounces the last line of the play when he calls down a malediction on the Travellers – the three malefactors fleeing off-stage, with the cry, "Run, run. Run for your lives" (1998, 50).

In a play such as Synge's, the Travellers are depicted as subverting all social proprieties, but their "inappropriate" behaviour is portrayed as more or less childlike and without malice. The action frequently plays like slapstick. This transgressive humour points to Synge's sympathy as a Protestant for the Traveller character's seemingly irreligious attitude as summed up by Mary's anticlericalism in her final speech to the priest, "[I]t's little need we ever had of the like of you to get us our bit to eat, and our bit to drink, and our time of love" (1998, 50). Understanding that comedy is a transgressive genre helps to mitigate the portrayal of Travellers as puckish, thieving, and unruly, particularly given that their ingenuous business acumen contrasts with the priest's more "mercenary" fixation on the meagreness of his payment. One of the possible effects of the staging of such a boundary-breaking play in a then-conservative society such as Ireland's was the potential for the audience to identify with the transgressors, in a kind of communal "disobedience"[44] or a symbolic "usurpation" of authority.

The main Traveller character in Sheridan's film (1990), the "tinker girl", represents a similar break from the stultifying expectations of a conservative and rural society, yet, the very fact that she is also nameless lends itself to the probability that she is a character type. Sheridan creates an exoticized representation of the "Bohemian Gypsy" girl, one which offers the fantasy of escape from repression (Sibley 1995, 15). The creation of such a fantasy construct, of course, assumes that outside the strictures of one's society equates with having no restrictions at all. Such a representation contradicts the traditional emphasis Travellers place on the ideal of chastity for young women, an emphasis which some scholars have

[44] Or there could be a backlash, such as the nationalist riots that followed the staging of Synge's *The Playboy of the Western World* in Dublin, 1907 (Cusack 2004).

provided as an explanation for early marriages for Travellers and other Gypsy peoples[45].

"Taking up" with the Traveller girl represents a radical break with both patriarchy and patrimony for Bull's son. At the fireside, the Traveller girl – who in earlier scenes had mocked Tadgh's slavishness to his father – notices his bruised face. These bruises, a consequence of the blows he received during his fight with the American, are, she supposes, the results of his father beating him. Her comment, "All fathers beat their children", reinforces the stereotype that is both the "violent" Irishman and the "patriarchal Traveller man". Wishing to impress her, Tadgh begins boasting and tells her that he has killed the "Yank". The next scene shows Tadgh and the Traveller girl sleeping in bed together.

Sheridan's film depicts the tinker girl as the catalyst for a chain of events that ultimately leads to the penultimate scene – one culminating in complete social and psychic rupture and devastation. Tadgh has decided to go away with the Traveller girl and goes with her the next day to bid his father farewell. The Bull calls the "tinker girl" a whore and informs Tadgh that she has betrayed them to the police with regard to the death of the "Yank". It is actually the girl's father, still aggrieved about his dead donkey, who has betrayed them. He has gone to the police with information concerning the killing of the "Yank"[46]. Tadgh does not renounce the girl, as expected, however, or his decision to go away with her. Instead, he reaffirms his decision to "run away" with her, thereby reinforcing his autonomy and his clear rejection of his father's values. "I never cared about the land", he tells Bull. This defiance on the part of Tadgh suggests that his decision to choose a Traveller wife is not an arbitrary one. Rather, it coincides with his decision to turn his back on the land and all it represents.

The Bull's warning to Tadgh in an early scene, "Never trust a woman who has no contact with the land," goes unheeded and Tadgh and the girl are seen driving away in her horse-drawn caravan. Interestingly, Tadgh is seen holding the reins as the couple fades from view, a gesture which indicates that he has found his "manhood" and is now playing an active role in his own destiny. Seeing that all he has worked for is lost and that he is powerless now to control events, the Bull "cracks", now losing his mind. The Bull's struggle has culminated in a failure of monumental

---

[45] Ed. note: In traditional Irish Traveller families, men are subject to virtually the same strictures with regard to talking to other women, sex outside marriage, arranged marriage etc.

[46] She does not deny that she told her father but there is no indication of ill-intent on her part.

proportions. At the end of the film, there are analogies between the Bull and the seminal, mythic figures, Cuchulainn and Canute (Herr 2002, 44), as we watch the now-deranged Bull drive his cattle towards a cliff with the intention of drowning them in the sea. Tadgh, who is already on the way out of the village, stops the wagon and at the girl's bidding, he runs to stop his father but instead is trampled by the stampeding cattle. Tadgh and the herd fall to their deaths.

The closing scene portrays Bull's wife and the Traveller girl standing at the top of the cliff, staring at the terrible carnage below. Maggie McCabe (Brenda Fricker) is seen stoically comforting the weeping Traveller girl[47]. The image of these two women surveying the total destruction of the Bull's "patriarchal" world suggests that their survival may be the instigation for a new communal society. On the shore below, the Bull stands waist-deep in seawater as he tries to hold back the crashing waves, slashing the surf with his ashplant. The mythic proportions of this tragic finale make allegorical interpretations unavoidable. It is as if the Bull represents narrow, rural, patriarchal tradition which is giving way to a "changing of the guard". Powerful a figure as the Bull is, even he is unable to hold back the inexorable tide of modernization. A sense of nostalgia pervades this scene and one can almost feel Sheridan's ambivalence with respect to the traditional patriarchal system he sees disappearing, a system that falls to the twofold impact of foreign economic dominance and pressures to modernize. The film's narrative betrays a strong sympathy for the rural life which is seen to be eroded by external forces. The ambivalent attitude towards modernization that characterizes the end of the film points to the tension created by pressures to abandon tradition (and patriarchy) and adopt "a forward-looking" (Herr 2002, 74) modernity that is equally frightening and unclear. Ambivalence toward modernity is evident in the emphasis on the significance of what has been lost. This double-mindedness reflects a mistrust in the values represented by the former colonizing power, Britain (also the world's first industrializing nation), as will be explored further in Part III of this volume. In this later section, Traveller writer Maher's (1998) apocryphal stories attribute a lack of religious fervour on the part of the "modern" Irish to Ireland's capitulation to the British "influence" and the "evils" of modernity.

[47] Notably, she does not shed a tear, as if her long acquaintance with sorrow (the suicide of her son) goes much deeper than spontaneous expressions of grief.

PART I

THE PROBLEM OF REPRESENTATION

In this section, we return to the Traveller narratives which are the focus of this volume. The hardships that Joyce endures correspond to a real life. Such representations raise a number of ethical issues since they are not merely aesthetic, but also contain "a moral dimension" (Eyerman 2001, 13). Eyerman (2001) insists that literary analysis must take this into account. Analysing an autobiography such as Joyce's, one written with the active political intention of promoting "a better understanding with the settled people" (Joyce 2000, 118), Part I of this volume examines not only the limitations of this text's language but also its dialogic possibilities. The problem of representation in Joyce's text raises the question: How can one best respond to negative representations within the "majority" community, representations which help to propagate stereotypes about Travellers and create difficulties between the Traveller and "settled" communities. Joyce often chooses the direct approach, one which scholars such as José Lanters (2005) find problematic. Close analysis makes clear that some of the difficulties actually are related to cultural differences as between "conventional" autobiography and Traveller self-representation – i.e., a kind of culture "clash" between the literary expectations of a reader encountering modes of oral expression as transposed to text. Finally, this section attempts to identify those elements of Traveller self-representation which operate most successfully, a particularly onerous venture given that such judgements must involve subjective criteria, to a large extent. As shall be demonstrated, however, even the most diligent of literary scholars approaches an oral text with a whole history / "baggage" of previous reading that never allows for an entirely unproblematic understanding of the text.

How others represent a group is not only crucial to that group's self-image but also affects how they are perceived (Dyer 1993, 1). Many Travellers are undoubtedly acutely aware of these negative representations, but to respond to them becomes a challenge for minority writers since the categories and terms of representation are always "codes and conventions of the available cultural forms … [that] set the wider terms of limitation and possibility" (Dyer 1993, 2). Familiar codes tend to be established by the dominant culture. Therefore, while everybody uses representations, minority cultures also sometimes must propose counter discourses that redefine what can be said while utilizing a shared language. Minority representations often counter dominant discourses by appropriating the language and images of the hegemonic culture. Recalling Roland Barthes' structuralist analysis of "the pure signifier, the empty signifier to which a multitude of meanings can be attached" (Barthes cited in Duncan and Duncan 1992, 22), the emptiness of certain cultural conventions can encompass a diversity, one which the minority writer can exploit, in order to generate creative alternatives to normal textual interpretations. For example, as will be examined below, Joyce employs an image familiar to her generation and to a presumed Irish Catholic audience / reader, the image of Mary, the Holy Mother, but she defamiliarizes the icon by transposing the image of motherhood into a more contemporary setting so that her reader might re-examine the degree to which a modern Ireland is committed to assuring that all Irish mothers, regardless of cultural or ethnic background, can raise their children in conditions that allow for their human dignity to remain intact. Thus, while representations can be used as an instrument of power, dominance and repression, counter discourses can also work to unbalance the power dynamic.

Much of this following section will address José Lanters' (2005) questions and misgivings in relation to Joyce's oral (narrative) style. Joyce's speaking / writing voice is directed outwards – as a dialogue. A dialogue always assumes a recipient or imaginary addressee, and implies the possibility of both response and communication. Her use of direct refutation, a popular tool in oratory, underlines the originally oral basis of argumentation, but can discomfit a reader / audience attuned to the more abstract argumentation which decades of literacy has engendered. In her essay (2005), "'We are a Different People': Life Writing, Representation, and the Travellers", Lanters claims that in Traveller writing, "explicit or implicit denials of negative stereotypes … often inadvertently perpetuate the stereotype by invoking it" (2005, 35). *My Life on the Road* (2000) opens by refuting the popular perception that Travellers are descendants of peasants displaced by the Famine who never managed to resettle, i.e., a narrative of "defeat". Joyce's rejoinder, "we're not drop-outs like some people think" (2000, 1), seems to be directed at an imaginary interlocutor. (Lanters' tendency to undervalue orality as a legitimate form of knowledge will be established in Part II).

Lanters (2005) begins her essay by looking at Joyce's frequent references to cleanliness, good habits which Joyce attributes to her upbringing. Joyce writes:

> Mother and Father had this thing for cleanness. Even though we only had an old wagon or tents in the summer everything had to be shining. The mugs might be washed perfectly clean but still a kettle of water would be boiled and thrown over them before Father would drink the tea. (2000, 4)

Joyce also mentions the importance of personal hygiene, "Mother was always bathing us and washing our hair. … Our hair used to be glittering" (2000, 4). By stressing the attention paid to the question of hygiene, Joyce refutes the strong association of Travellers with dirt, a belief that corresponds with a long-standing "bourgeois" abhorrence of poverty[1].

The detail Joyce pays to this question of cleanliness may seem defensive only if it is considered as a rejoinder to negative appellations or stereotypes, but the above quote is also informational, containing hints of Traveller proscriptions in relation to hygiene and pollution. Ironically, in view of the proliferation of non-Traveller rhetoric that associates Travellers with dirt, some Travellers consider their settled neighbours to be unclean (see Helleiner, 2000). Traveller and Gypsy purity beliefs focus on notions of pollution and purity as inferred in Joyce's description of rinsing already clean-teacups. Taboos centre on maintaining strict separation between the outer body and the inner body (Okely 1983, 78-87)[2]. Anything can potentially pollute the inner body if separation practices have not been strictly adhered to. This includes not only food, but also anything that touches food, such as dishes, utensils and food containers. Several washbasins are kept for different, exclusive purposes (Okely 1983, 81). A kitchen sink is never used to wash hands, clothes or hair, for example. In some modern Traveller trailers and motor homes, kitchen sinks are boarded up or never installed (Okely 1983, 82). Even kitchen linens are washed separately in basins that have never been used for general washing and hung to dry apart from other linens and clothes. Joyce (2000) relates that even as young children they were aware of these prohibitions:

---

[1] Dirt is connected with poverty (Sibley 1995, 57-8), and with a racist association of darker skinned people (Roma, East Indians, Africans, etc.) (Sibley 1995, 22-4).

[2] Okely (1983) studied cleanliness taboos among English 'Traveller-Gypsies', but Ní Shúinéar (1994) notes that these beliefs are also observed among some Irish Travellers (1994, 56).

> When we were growing up we had this thing about cleanness and if we were out in the day we wouldn't ask tea until we came to a real clean house. ... If we saw a woman in a house with dirty nails or teeth we wouldn't ask for tea. ... We'd never drink out of a stranger's cup and when the woman would be making us tea we'd say, "Now put it in a bottle" – we thought it would be cleaner than cups because nobody ever drank out of the bottle. (2000, 24-5)

These taboos are a barrier which ensure a separation between Traveller / Gypsy and non-Traveller communities, thus helping to preserve the integrity of an endogamous people (Okely 1983, 80). Joyce provides perspectives on issues of contention that have often been ignored, thereby initiating a dialogue which can work towards inter-cultural understanding. In practical terms, knowledge about cultural differences can avoid misunderstandings such as have sometimes occurred in the design of "official" Traveller campsites where the washing facilities were located in the same building as the toilets, for example.

Joyce's stated purpose in writing is to increase understanding between communities, but this in no way includes the desire to assimilate (or be assimilated) into "mainstream" culture. In fact, her implicit argument throughout her book is the opposite of this, i.e., that Travellers should not have to give up their culture in order to find acceptance and equality within Ireland. Lanters (2005), on the other hand, seems to consider any highlighting of "difference" as perpetuating the terms of social exclusion. She writes, "The very strategies that are meant to reduce the marginal status of a minority group often have the opposite effect, merely by the act of drawing attention to the otherness of that group" (Lanters 2005, 33). Here, Lanters conflates an externally-imposed segregation that views difference as aberrant and threatening with a strategy such as Joyce's which proposes difference as non-threatening and seeks to build on commonalities between communities. Along with an appeal for a greater tolerance of difference, Joyce and other Traveller writers (see Cawley, 2004; Dunne, 2004) confirm their uniqueness as a point of pride even as they attempt to create a self-image that challenges negative images as imposed by others. Her conclusion, "we are a different people" (2000, 118), encapsulates her pride in her Traveller identity and her sustained position that difference should not be a reason to deny Travellers' rights to equal citizenship in Ireland.

Lanters questioning of a process of direct refutation is related to her ambivalence with regard to the "bigger question" that is the issue of representation itself. She hints in her opening paragraph that the failure inherent in aspects of Joyce's writing may lie in Joyce's process of "representation" but also she questions "the very notion of representation itself" (Lanters 2005, 25). She eventually circumvents this issue by interiorising Joyce's project, an interpretation that appears to run counter to Joyce's purpose of addressing the external conditions Travellers face and educating (the reading) public. Lanters' analysis places a strong emphasis on the individual and suggests that Traveller "life writing, while ostensibly aimed at influencing the attitude of a settled audience, may effect greater changes in the writers themselves" (2005, 41). Such an analysis hints at a partial failure in the writer's conscious intentions, yet allows for Traveller writing as a creative process which helps the writer construct "'a *sustainable self-image*" (Gullestad, cited and italicized in Lanters 2005, 41). Lanters disassociates the act of writing from the kind of intersubjective reader response an editor such as Elizabeth Laing (1992) hoped for[3] by the preface to *Moving Stories: Traveller Women Write*, to a more self-contained role whereby the individual writes in order to define himself / herself. Lanters' emphasis on autobiographical writing as an individual process rather than a communal one diminishes its dialogic potential, and reflects the "traditional", modern Western approach, based on the isolated and interiorised Cartesian self. In contrast, Joyce's discomfort with personal disclosures and her preference for remaining in the background of her story while foregrounding the circumstances then common to many Travellers indicates a less individualistic and more communal sense of identity that has been remarked in minority and women's autobiographies (Friedman 1988, 34; Gilmore 1994, 77). Lanters' emphasis on the individual's self-image, while valid, must be understood within the context of the more communal self-identity that is evident in Traveller writing. Lanters is correct in concluding that one of the functions of autobiography is the process of creating "sustainable" self-definitions for the writer, a role that is not an exclusive one, however.

While Joyce's responses to the oppression of the Traveller community can sometimes appear defensive, other strategies of hers disarm these reservations, her use of humour and her customary optimism, for instance. Perhaps more than any other narrative technique, it is her skillful characterizations of three of the key people in her life which help counter stereotypes and personalize the sweeping nature of the anti-Traveller generalizations and bigotry. The difficulty of finding a shared language,

---

[3] In the preface, Laing writes, "The candour of these writings and their expectations of a response made in friendship challenges the reader to respond in that way. The reader is involved personally, intersubjectively, and thereby understanding is increased" (Laing 1992, 7).

one which does not reiterate the oppressive nature of the dominant culture, is Joyce's unique challenge.

Although Joyce does sometimes fall back on generalizations when portraying both Travellers and non-Travellers, those anecdotes that depict Travellers and non-Travellers as individuals are far more convincing and effective in challenging stereotypes. Fond memories from Joyce's childhood illustrate Traveller family life in positive terms. In the anecdotes of her early years, she develops three main characters, i.e., her father, her older sister Kathleen and her younger brother Willie. Gusdorf's (1912-2000) claim that "autobiographical selves are constructed through the process of writing and therefore cannot reproduce exactly the selves who lived" (Gusdorf cited in Friedman 1988, 34), also applies to the "characters" populating both Joyce's and Maher's autobiographies, even if they represent actual people. In Joyce (2000), character development is drawn through the use of various literary techniques, (occasionally) through direct appraisal by the authorial voice, but most often through the incorporation of anecdote.

Joyce's many stories about her father counter the frequent negative stereotypes of Traveller men as violent and feckless by showing him to be a role model. She underlines his strong sense of pride in his heritage, a sense of self-worth she inherits, and which comes to fruition as her leadership role in the Traveller community evolves. Whether intentional or not, Joyce's statement, "The way he dressed people never took him for a traveller but he used to make a point of telling them because he never was ashamed of it" (2000, 6), tends to set her father apart as "exceptional" from other Travellers. Countering those long-held stereotypes which portray Travellers as lazy, Joyce describes the care and meticulousness with which her father would build and decorate Traveller wagons[4], a specialized skill not widely practiced even then. Besides focusing on the many ways her father earned a living for the family, she describes the vital role Travellers served as skilled craftsmen and traders within the rural Irish economy and the good relations they shared with settled people when she was young:

> Ireland was very poor then … you couldn't get copper or brass or tin or anything like that so the travellers used to smuggle it in their wagons. They'd bring it into the Free State [The Republic] … and they'd make tins and pots and lovely copper ornaments and buckets. In those days

[4] Ward, Joyce's sister, mentions that some of these wagons were made to order for a wider Traveller clientele (Ward 1992, 60).

> travellers were *different*; they were a very proud people. (My emphasis, Joyce, 2000, 3)

Joyce's example counters popular and long-held stereotypes that depict Travellers as social welfare "scroungers" and yet, her discussion of economic autonomy as relating to a previous era seems to confirm rather than dispel views such as those found in Gmelch's (1985) study. This study claimed that "while 'itinerants' had once had a viable rural lifestyle, modernization made their skills redundant" (Gmelch cited in Ní Shúinéar 2002, 186). Joyce would certainly not have wanted to put forward nomadism, and therefore Travellers, as anachronisms, as she almost appears to suggest. By making this comparison, she does establish that disparities in the levels of Traveller self-sufficiency are not due to any innate "defects" in the Traveller character. Since Traveller writers almost unanimously assert that living conditions and relations between the "settled" and Travelling communities have deteriorated within the past few decades, the unfavourable comparison between past and present raises the question of discontinuity and rapid social change. Worsening economic conditions for Travellers will be examined in Part III of this volume as an element in the anti-modernist discourse as expressed by Maher. Here it will be noted that despite publishing in 1985, Joyce's emphasis on class issues as "dividing practices" in Irish society anticipated to a certain degree the effect of the "Celtic Tiger" economy that Ireland experienced in the 1990s, an economic boom that brought prosperity but also permitted wide economic disparities. In contemporary Ireland, as elsewhere, definitions of "class" are often based on income. While Locke (1632-1704) equated good citizenship with the ownership of private property, Merriman (1999) notes that in a globalizing economy, "[i]nclusion in the social order is … predicated on economic capital, disposable income and lifestyle" (1999, 311), all criteria which assure the exclusion of the poor.

While Joyce can only rarely be suspected of (deliberately) choosing words which evoke sympathy, neither is she naïve. Her powerful rhetorical skills have given her a confident sense of the emotional impact which words can carry. Generally, her vignettes convey a spontaneous warmth, even as they contradict negative stereotypes. At the same time, an acute sensitivity to commonly-cited, reductionist stereotypes can provoke "defensive" responses. For example, she details the various ways in which her father made a living, including horse training and breeding purebred dogs, and immediately adds, "He never used to hit a horse or let anyone be cruel to animals" (2000, 6), thereby, refuting stereotypes which depict Travellers as more apt to mistreat animals. Such counter-discourses demonstrate the fact that, while writing, Travellers are always cognisant of the negative stereotypes they are writing against.

Other anecdotes reveal a thirst for knowledge, "inquiring minds" which contradict those stereotypes which would depict Travellers as ignorant by nature[5]. Joyce's father conducted formal lessons in the evening by the light of the gas lamp, teaching by rote, a technique derived from oral tradition and long-retained as a pedagogic tool in literate societies. Besides learning their alphabet, much attention also focused on the Traveller children's religious education. Joyce mentions the "little sally rod about as thick as a match" that her father used during these lessons, "he'd be waving it. It was springy and if you got it across the legs you'd really feel it" (2000, 20). Though typical of the methods used in classrooms of the era and meant as a humorous comment, Joyce nevertheless feels the need to offset any suspicions amongst her readers by adding, "My father never battered us, he'd never hit us hard, but while he was teaching us the catechism we'd be looking at this sally rod, going" (2000, 20).

While Joyce's mother remains (for the most part) a silence in the text, her father appears in most of the anecdotes concerning her early life and is also strongly associated with the happiest times of her early life. The tragedy of his untimely death – he died while in police custody, a death never subjected to any official investigation – is felt more strongly by the careful reader since Joyce has taken great care to reveal his character. Admittedly, considering the sudden and violent way in which her father was taken from them, Joyce's portrait of him may be somewhat idealized. However, given the obvious affection with which she remembers her father, it would be too cynical to suggest that her descriptions of his industriousness and resourcefulness are a "defensive" ploy designed to counter negative stereotypes. Regretting his early death, she often hints that had he survived, their entire family would have had a happier life. On several occasions she attributes her lack of education to his early death such as when she says, "my father died when we were very young and he

---

[5] Such beliefs can manifest themselves as discriminatory practices. Many Traveller autobiographies testify that Travellers were treated differently in the school system, not only that they were subjected to racist comments by teachers and students alike, but that teachers did not bother to try to teach them the regular school curriculum. One writer, Bridget Gaffey (1992) says, "when all the girls were learning Maths, English, Irish, and History, I was always given a colouring book to go to the back of the class while all the other girls of the settled community did the work. They never tried to teach me any of the things I would have loved to have done" (Gaffey 1992, 92-3).

didn't get much time to teach us" (2000, 21). At one point, Joyce reminisces, poignantly – "when Father was alive we were so happy" (2000, 67). Meyer Spacks notices a tendency in women autobiographers to look back on childhood as "often the happiest and freest time", and suggests that this nostalgia hints at the "loss of self" adulthood can represent for some women, particularly for many women of Joyce's generation living in often-patriarchal societies: "[T]herefore", Spacks writes, such women "[look] back fondly to the relative freedom and power of childhood and youth" (Spacks cited in Heilbrun 1988, 72). The occasional glimpses of Nan Joyce's then marital problems reinforce Spacks's view and may explain the lighter tone and "spirit of adventure" that permeates all but the most despondent moments in Joyce's childhood accounts. Joyce offers another explanation[6] – the complete trust she was able to place in her older sister Kathleen while their mother was in prison. When Kathleen left the family – i.e., three months before their mother's release – Joyce admits that she became depressed (2000, 51). Having so recently lost their father, and with their mother in prison, Joyce experienced her sister's departure as yet another loss, one made all the more difficult because of their vulnerable situation. Her admission that while Kathleen was with them "we had a big person to lean on" (2000, 51) suggests that, even when times are difficult, the sense of mutual support gained from shared responsibilities provides courage and strength, a reciprocity that appears to be absent in her account of her adult life.

The warm sense of humour in her accounts of the early years helps to offset the harsh life circumstances described. Her humour is disarming, although it sometimes feels like an attempt to put forward the most optimistic conclusion possible, in the circumstances. Humour can also serve as a defence mechanism. For example, her quip when the police officers tell her that her husband is "sleeping it off" in the cell – "'Oh, great, he might be sobered now'" (94), seems like one such an instance. Her use of humour to downplay negative behaviour as related to excessive drinking attempts to deflect any criticism by asserting that this drinking has few serious or lasting consequences. Joyce uses the example of fairs, a combined social / business activity that once represented an important source of income for Traveller families, as well as a hub of social contacts. Joyce observes that if they drank too much during business transactions, "the men who had the new wagons might end up with the rotten ones … But they usen't to worry about it because the next time at the fair they'd be

[6] This is not to invalidate Spacks's observation.

a lot wiser" (14-15). Physical brawls were then little more than "a letting-off of steam" with no real lasting animosity between warring parties[7]:

> When the men were drunk they might have a boxing match but they'd fall more times than they'd hit each other. Next morning they'd have a black eye each and they'd be ashamed to get out of bed to face each other … And then the two men that were boxing would shake hands – they never kept in any spite or hate … Then the women would march them to the priest to take the pledge. (2000, 18)

Her depiction is, in a sense, cartoon-like, almost slapstick in nature. In a motif familiar to Irish literature, it is the women who take matters in hand. The men are portrayed as childlike, thereby carrying on the cliché of the strong woman and the physically virile, but morally-weak man, now the submissive penitent. Sometimes rendered tragically, here the scene is almost comical: "[T]he men would be brought to the priest and they'd let on to be real innocent saying, 'Oh, Father, we didn't mean to fight'" (2000, 18). While Joyce refuses to judge or condemn their behaviour, she admits that life was better for everyone when they were not drinking: "When the men had taken the pledge you'd see the change in them in a few days" (2000, 18).

Both Joyce and Maher contextualize the social and economic conditions that frame the social problems of certain Traveller families / individuals, thereby drawing a relation between despair, alcoholism and discriminatory practices, a strategy which proves a very effective one. Unlike Joyce (2000) who seems to address a reader / listener, Maher's (1998) frequent insights into his childhood reveal a more self-reflective attempt on the part of an adult who is now writing in order to arrive at a personal understanding of his own human nature. Whether through the act of writing itself or with the wisdom gained in the intervening years, Maher later comes to view his father's harsh and cruel behaviour with compassion, an evolution that also influences the reader's understanding of the text. Maher's candid account of the problem of alcoholism within his family is much grimmer than Joyce's and provides a counterpoint to her "caricature-type" descriptions and reticence about how the problem has affected her personal life. His tone is a darker one with more stress laid on the negative impacts of physical and verbal abuse. Maher introduces the reality of his troubled childhood on the very first page of his

---

[7] Maria Campbell, in her "life story", *Half-breed*, uses a similar strategy to counter outsider views. Describing her Métis childhood, Campbell writes of their social life, "We never had a dance without a good fight and we enjoyed and looked forward to it as much as the dancing" (Campbell 1973, 57).

book. His second sentence, "My father, when sober …", immediately highlights his father's alcoholism, which he describes as follows: "My father was a character, a real hard case, a man who lived for a drink" (1998, 9). He characterizes his mother's teetotalism as "a rare thing on the road" (1998, 9), which suggests drinking as a norm among certain Traveller families back then and also serves to reinforce her exceptional moral character.

When portraying the verbal tongue-lashings and physical beatings he suffered at the hands of his father, Maher is unflinching in his descriptions. In those circumstances where he is a more detached observer, however, i.e., when the situation involves others and not his mother and himself, he occasionally downplays the extent of the physical violence or beatings. His minimizing of the harmful effects of conflict as "all soon forgotten" (1998, 21), contradicts his earlier assertion that witnessing parental conflict has a very detrimental effect on children: "I always felt distressed when my parents started to fight with each other … Seeing this when one is young, during the formative … years of one's life, does no real good; in fact, more often than not it destroys" (1998, 19). Maher goes on to describe the destructive effect interpersonal conflict can have on children. He writes: "In the end the child can only continue as his parents did before him" (1998, 19) – a statement which suggests a certain inevitability in the perpetuation of negative or inappropriate behaviour. Maher's shifting positions on these questions underline the difficulty of his in-between "cultural" status and recall Lanters' reference to "conflicting loyalties". The tensions inherent in attempting to integrate multiple positions can result in a form of psychological splitting. In Maher (1998), alternating views are most often articulated through the mouths of his characters, a tactic that permits the writer the freedom to explore contradictory opinions without having to take a completely definitive stance. In Maher's case, his ambivalence may not only be due to an intercultural conflict but may also be due to both intercultural and familial loyalties.

On a larger scale, Maher portrays the various conflicts and misunderstandings between Travellers and non-Travellers as a consequence of a fundamental culture clash. Disagreements arise because the different communities have different needs. This corroborates McVeigh's assertion that nomadic and sedentary people "stand in a contradictory relationship because they occupy the same social space in a profoundly different way" (1997, 22). One example of this is recycling, an economic activity which functions as an important source of income for Travellers. In Maher's day,

Travellers would collect and recycle everything from bottles and rags to scrap metal.

The second occasion his family tried to settle in a house, Maher describes the attempt as a "great trial for my parents … We found it almost impossible to adapt to it" (1998, 139). Because his father worked in recycling, junk began to accumulate inside the house and outside, "old rags, horse-hair, feathers and … scrap" (1998, 139). Because he inhabits an in-between-place, Maher is able to see why "settled" people are angry because of these practices while at the same time, he understands the Traveller perspective. He describes the house as "a dump", and considers the neighbours' complaints as "natural", but he also sees the harm the conflict had for his brothers and sisters who suffered jeers from the settled children in the neighbourhood and at school, an ordeal which resulted in their frequent absences from school. Furthermore, he concludes that his mother "took the full brunt of all this … worry" because his father could "go out and have a few drinks to ease his mind" (1998, 140). Maher describes his mother's social isolation in an earlier unsuccessful attempt to settle in a house when he was eight years old. Maher attributes their ostracism to a general hostility towards Travellers:

> [W]e were not wanted; there was always a great deal of prejudice among the townspeople … [My mother] was always alone in the house; none of the neighbours would even talk to her, let alone come into our house for a visit or a cup of tea. To the townspeople we were dirty, begging tinkers and no respectable person would visit us. (My emphasis 1998, 17)

Again, Maher depicts his mother as the one who bore the heaviest burden because of her social role as a stay-at-home mother with no income. The moral overtones of social exclusion are contained in Maher's qualification that it was "respectable" society that shunned them.

In these difficult circumstances, he identifies the "arguments and quarrels" that ensued between his parents as "only natural" (1998, 19), given that external pressures can put strains on personal relations. This comprehension, however, is the insight of the adult writer. Elsewhere, Maher states that as children witnessing these battles, they were "puzzl[ed], for we could not understand" (1998, 19). When they decided to leave the first house they lived in, Seán cried, and this caused a row between his parents. It is only at the beginning of the next chapter and immediately subsequent to the story of the Traveller woman who is beaten by her husband detailed below that Maher reveals not only that his father had struck him but also the source of his father's frustration: "I remember with deep resentment the punch I got from my father that day we left our little house. I cried because I didn't want to leave and he punched me, *I feel now*, because he really didn't want to leave either" (my italics 1998, 23). Maher does not make excuses for his father's action, but Maher, the adult writer now believes he understands something of his father's emotional state at this time. Maher pinpoints the cause of his father's sometimes violent behaviour as an unresolved and (perhaps) irresolvable internal conflict, his father's inability to face his own sense of vulnerability and his impotence in the face of those obstacles in his life which he cannot seem to change. Maher's novelistic technique of detailed and (slightly-fictionalized) conversations between his parents reveals the underlying sense of failure that haunts his father. As they hit the road once more, his father denies having any regrets, "It's just as well we left that town, I got sick of the place" (1998, 18), and equates living in town with "sheer starvation" (1998, 18). To this, Maher adds: "My father, of course, felt it very deeply, living in a town and not being able to get a day's work. Living on a few measly shillings' relief was no joke" (1998, 18). Maher also observes that the futility of his father's many efforts to provide for his family left his father "often depressed" (1998, 19). These are the first hints of a new and more complex understanding that Maher, the adult writer outlines. His father cannot really cope with their marginalized societal position and responds by lashing out at his own family. The backdrop of general antipathy towards Travellers helps Maher to explain (without excusing) his father's verbal and physical violence.

Maher intersperses the bleakness of these early years with humorous stories, thereby providing frequent shifts in the narrative tone. Though he looks for the humour in situations, at the end of chapter one, he tries unconvincingly to make light of an incident that begins as a practical joke, but ends with the wife of another couple being severely beaten. The couple's dispute underlines the demands imposed within a very patriarchal society – the row was precipitated by a ruined supper. Although Maher describes a horrific beating, where the husband "caught hold of his wife by the hair with one hand and punched her repeatedly in the face with the other", he then downplays the effects of the row: "The next morning the row was forgotten" (1998, 22). The child witnessing the scene and the present writing "self" are one and the same. Neither has forgotten that: "Maggie's face was battered and scarred and swollen, so much so that she had to remain in bed for about a week after" (1998, 22). Maher the writer concludes his description of this incident and chapter one as a whole by declaring, "There is great cruelty on the road, but then again there is great love and kindredship among travellers that overcomes all hardships" (1998, 22). This declaration is a problematic one since Maher himself surmounts his own personal difficulties only sporadically and only after hard-fought personal struggles. Maher's accomplishments are intermeshed with moments of desperate loneliness and even despair. As with Joyce's autobiography, there is a sense here that Maher's use of "concluding" statements is meant to convince the writer as much as the reader.

By framing his family's misery within a larger context, Maher implies a collective responsibility yet does not pontificate or jump to judgement. He explores these enlarged perspectives through his characters. He begins to see his father not only as a victimizer, but also as one of life's casualties; a man who is unable to cope with the difficulties of an overtly-hostile society without the crutch that is alcohol. In the penultimate chapter of his autobiography, Maher, who is, by now a young man on his own, views his father's alcoholism in empathetic terms – a vehicle for human frailty. He arrives at this conclusion just as he is arguing with two fellow Travellers on the merit of the traditional travelling life. In contrast to the other two men, Maher argues against nomadism, and pauses in the debate to muse, "I thought of my father trying to drink himself out of his misery and into a better, if imaginary, life" (1998, 154). This reflection casts a new light on his father's physical violence, depicting him as a man caught in his own personal anguish, a pain that he, in turn, inflicts on others. Maher's candour offers a harsh perspective on Traveller life, one that would appear, on first glance, to corroborate long-held anti-Traveller stereotypes. His ability to weave in external causes resituates the story from a personal tragedy to failure on a larger and more human level. Through Maher's eyes, the reader begins not only to comprehend the tragedy of "wasted" lives, but also to look beyond individual action and personal responsibility to the social conditions that can function to limit individual choice (Hirschmann 2003, 20-23).

Maher's writing portrays a man / writer on a personal journey to self-discovery, a path where forgiveness opens the way to liberation from a difficult childhood. Maher expresses this new beginning in the concluding pages of his book. His proverbial "life is a journey" trope that evokes the long-established Christian tradition of pilgrimage resonates with his Traveller identity, which Maher symbolically shares with the reader by reminding him / her that we are all travellers on that road (1998, 165). Borrowing such recognizable images and reshaping them to express a distinct perspective, one which is familiar yet unique, highlights the flexibility of these easily recognizable cultural images.

Joyce's writing also makes a powerful impact when she puts forward simple but redolent images, portraits in miniature which evoke the familiar and yet set it slightly askew. One such image occurs in the anecdote about

Joyce's elder sister Kathleen who went missing one day and was found by her parents "in the middle of the Corporation dump in Whiterock and every bit was covered in ashes. She was sitting there like a fairy reading Dandys and Beanos — that was how she learned to read, from the comics" (2000, 31-2). This single image encompasses a range of interrelations. Firstly, this portrait refutes the long-held stereotype that associates Travellers with ignorance and a lack of education. "Like a fairy," suggests a pleasant scene, one which is not meant to arouse pity, and yet illustrates the courage and determination which children demonstrate, even when growing up in difficult societal conditions. Kathleen, sitting in the rubbish, reading her Beanos also evokes contemporary images of those children and their families who make their living sifting through mountains of garbage at landfill sites, collecting recyclable materials to sell (an activity that continues to supplement Traveller income (Helleiner 145-9)). This snapshot also bears testimony to the practice of relegating marginalized peoples to peripheral locations on the edges of society. Because "power is expressed in the monopolization of space and the relegation of weaker groups in society to less desirable environments" (Sibley 1995, ix), landfill sites become a potent geographic symbol of ownership claims and out-group apartheid[8]. As if symbolizing their pariah status, the "undesirable" elements of society live in closer proximity to the mountain of waste that is created by affluence than those people who can afford to live in safer environments. By presenting a familiar image – the happy, inquisitive child – and then displacing it (i.e., her classroom is a rubbish dump and her reading materials are cast-offs), Joyce undercuts any sentimentality.

In a similar fashion, but more consciously perhaps, Joyce reworks an iconic Catholic symbol. Manipulating familiar images in ways which question the underlying beliefs that empower the motif provides one solution to the problem of language constraints. In the final chapter, "A Better Understanding", Joyce returns to a memory from her childhood. Just as she once associated her father with an idyllic happiness, Joyce also appears to associate her mother with hardship and lack. Joyce remembers a cold winter's day when she and her mother had been out begging – an

[8] In Eastern Canada, Africville, a century old African-Canadian community established on land beside Halifax harbour was subjected to a municipal rubbish dump and other spatial harassments located in their community. Their community was bulldozed out of existence in 1967 and replaced by a harbour front park (Mackenzie 1991). These disputed lands – so called "squatter" or "shanty" towns are a growing phenomenon worldwide – creating a legal limbo for residents whose sometimes decades long "occupation" rather than official legal status (deeds) is their only claim to ownership.

activity which Joyce depicts as a form of humiliation. On this particular day, Joyce feels the sting of rejection to a greater extent than normal – "people kept banging the doors in our faces" (2000, 117). She notices that even those people who gave them something "wouldn't speak to us" (2000, 117). Joyce and her mother went into a chapel to warm themselves where, Joyce likens her mother, "praying with the child in her arms", to a statue in the chapel of "Our Lady with the Child Jesus in a sort of shawl" (2000, 117) – the shawl being a once-traditional covering for Traveller women. By superimposing the image of her mother and the Holy Mother, Joyce tends towards the maudlin, but then she grounds herself in the moment again by describing the child Nan[9] as a child who "wonder[s] why people should be treated like this" (2000, 117). Whether it is the adult writer or the child who remembers – the conclusion is one and the same, i.e., the Travellers "weren't real people to them" (2000, 117). Ironically, it may be that the Travellers were too "real", too "close", or too associated with the past that the Irish people have left behind – the endemic poverty, the evictions, the Famine, the history of colonization. It may be that proximity induces fear and loathing. Sibley (1995) argues that when nomadism can be placed in a safely distant past, Roma and Travellers can then be seen in the miasma of a pastoral idyll, but only if the image stays far removed in time and place. The child's avowal *not* to grow up to be like her mother – "'I'll make a better life when I grow up – I won't have to beg, I won't have to be pitiful-looking to get charity just to survive'" (2000, 117) – shatters the idealism that is the iconic image.

Such repudiations are indicative of the mother's apparent inferior status, a perception that reflects the lack of regard given to her role in society. Siegel (2001) notes that in women's autobiography, "The mother—typically—does not present a model whose power exceeds the domestic sphere" (2001, 21). Siegel's analysis is corroborated in Joyce's emphasis on her father in descriptions of her childhood. The dissimilar textual treatment allotted to her mother suggests that while she may have loved her mother, she may not have viewed her mother as someone she wished to emulate, an assessment which may reflect the societal values of this era when the household and care-giving responsibilities traditionally performed by women were completely undervalued and uncelebrated. The contrast is accentuated by the manner whereby Joyce highlights the difference between her two parents. Concerning her mother's lack of education, Joyce states, "My mother couldn't read or write, she never had

---

[9] The placement of the thought within the young child's cognizance makes the recognition of maltreatment more poignant.

any education and I think she felt a bit left out because my father was such a scholar" (2000, 6). Likewise, the more perfunctory treatment of her mother's activities contrasts with the rich and varied sensations her father's activities elicit – such as her description of him shoeing horses: "He'd … redden the horseshoe in the fire. Steam and smoke would come out when he put the shoe on the hoof but it didn't hurt the horse. I used to love the smell of the horse's hooves scorching" (2000, 6). Although she mentions her mother's fresh baked bread, there is none of the heightened senses or enthrallment associated with her father's work. It is worth noting that Joyce grew up in a very "traditional" Irish society, one where, whether Traveller or non-Traveller, the public domain was considered a male realm and a woman's place was in the home. Joyce's move into the public sphere in later life when working as a Traveller advocate and social activist (and running for public office), highlights the strong connection she felt with her father and his more exciting sphere of action, especially given that he was her apparent role model.

It must be noted that the sharp delineation of gender roles in Joyce's account was a cultural norm in Ireland and other "Western" countries at the time. Joyce's implied question – "Did I make a better life?" – is not merely a self-reflective one given that the conditions on evaluation are based on a hegemonic consensus which repudiates certain groups and individuals. Joyce challenges these mainstream values when she places emphasis on the moral qualities of each human being as opposed to the question of personal achievement. She asserts in the Afterword to her book, "I'm not ashamed of my children, they're all good; they're not rich but they have their goodness and pity and charity—that's the main thing" (2000, xii). In adding, "[T]hey're not rich," she calls attention to the tendency in capitalist societies to measure a person's value solely in a monetary sense. She extends this sense of self-worth to her own abilities, but acknowledges that all may not share her standards: "Settled people would look at you as an uneducated person but I've been highly educated in cooking, looking after children and managing" (2000, xii). Her point concurs with one that many feminists have tried to make: work traditionally done by women has also been frequently undervalued.

Joyce's challenge is to find a language that the majority culture can understand and even connect with as "their own", but one which does not misrepresent her averred views and values. Such a contradiction occurs when Joyce speaks of her sister Kathleen's success. Being the eldest, Kathleen is only fourteen when the children are left without their parents and she takes on many of the responsibilities for keeping the family together during that difficult period. Thinking that her mother had served her time and was about to be released from prison[10], Kathleen left the other children and made her way to England, where she did quite well eventually. When celebrating Kathleen's life and marriage, Joyce adopts a language which assumes "majority" values and attaches importance to social status, a view which contradicts her earlier arguments against social class as a determinant of human worth. Although Joyce's praise of her sister is without any obvious irony, she does attempt to contextualize the appearance of success by wondering, "What kind of life must she have had?" (2000, 51, 63). Without answering this question, Joyce nevertheless underlines the obstacles Kathleen must have faced when, aged just fifteen, she went alone to England – where "she had no-one there to go to … no money, no education" (2000, 51). Although Joyce does not presume to analyze the interior lives of others or speak "on their behalf", the first time she meets her sister again – in Glasgow some four years later – Joyce comments on Kathleen's style: "She'd turned into a lovely lady, you'd think she was from a big posh house the way she was dressed and the way she had her hair" (2000, 63). Especially important in a society where one's accent can prevent upward mobility, Kathleen had learned to speak "real English" (2000, 63). However, Joyce concludes that "the happy person Kathleen had been was there no more" (2000, 63). The reader is left to imagine the contradictions or "concessions" Kathleen has had to make in order to fit into a lifestyle so foreign to her upbringing. Joyce recounts an amusing anecdote when Kathleen would rearrange the furniture in her house, "The way settled men are they have their favourite armchair and [Kathleen's husband] he'd be looking for it to sit down … and she'd say 'Well, I've shifted today!' The traveller was still in her after all those years!" (2000, 67).

Kathleen's success has been achieved through cultural assimilation, having married an educated, "settled" man. Joyce describes a "success" story that portrays the abandonment of the customs and culture of one's birth to adopt a "settled" lifestyle, although her autobiography argues throughout that Travellers should not have to give up their culture in order to fully participate in society. Momentarily slipping into a language that adopts "majority" values after having asserted Traveller values as different, less materialistic, or more humane etc., Joyce's account reflects the personal inconsistencies and contradictions common to all language users[11]. Some of Joyce's difficulty here arises from having to create a

---

[10] In fact, Joyce's mother had to serve an additional three months for unpaid illegal camping fines.

[11] The more far-reaching and long-term the project, the more susceptible rhetorical belief systems become to inconsistency. Fraser, for one, criticizes Foucault for

language that responds to hegemonic standards that are proposed as cultural "norms" while simultaneously asserting Traveller cultural differences as both reconcilable with, and complementary to the values of the "majority" Irish community.

Examining the ways whereby the conscious intention of a speaker / writer can be destabilized by contradictory subtexts provides various insights into how direct discourses function, not only their ability to communicate specific issues, but also as regards those language "lapses" which create ambiguity. This latter occurrence, when it appears, underlines the ambivalence produced by the "'conflicting loyalties'" (Seyhan cited in Lanters 2005, 38) of straddling two cultures, and the difficulties for the minority culture of negotiating and creating a meaningful place within the larger society. Ambiguity need not be perceived as a failure of technique since the implications of contradictory interpretations direct the reader outwards and back to the circumstances which inform the writing / speaking voice. Such approaches thus demand the type of intersubjective readings which Traveller writers wish to encourage through the telling of their stories. Representations, in general, are "imperfect" in scope since they are imbued with conventional, uncritically accepted ideologies inherent to the cultural milieu from which they emerge. Alternative perspectives such as those which Traveller writers present enlarge the terms and categories of representation and consequently should not to be dismissed as having subjective (i.e., individualistic) implications, solely.

Minority discourses face the difficulty of redefining and "retelling" elements of the dominant discourse. To this end, Part II of this volume examines how Traveller writers and storytellers rewrite foundational Irish mythologies in order to reconfigure the terms of representation which cast Travellers as historical "victims". Their versions of well-known apocryphal stories portray Travellers as agents of history in active and participatory roles which support Traveller claims to a longstanding presence in Ireland and their rights to full citizenship. In the process, they argue that orality is a valid means of transmitting their ancestral

---

depending on Enlightenment values "for the force of his arguments" while simultaneously undermining these values, but concedes that part of the difficulty of his task lies in the challenge of having to create an entirely new language:

> The fact that Foucault continues to speak … the language of humanism need not be held against him. Every good Derridean will allow that there is not, at least for the time being, any other language he could speak … Foucault himself acknowledges that he cannot simply and straightaway discard at will the normative notions associated with the metaphysics of subjectivity. (Fraser 1989, 57)

knowledge. Their approach to history as story-making thus provides imaginative alternatives to hegemonic discourses which may claim to be the only valid representations of history.

PART II

ALTERNATIVE HISTORY: WRITING TRAVELLERS INTO THE NATION'S DISCOURSE

> except that it is not a story,
> more a rumour or a folk memory
> …
>
> there is a way of making free with the past,
> a pastiche of what is
> real and what is
> not, which can only be
> justified if you think of it
>
> not as sculpture but syntax:
>
> a structure extrinsic to meaning which uncovers
> the inner secret of it.
>
> —"Lava Cameo", Eavan Boland

Autobiography demands re-membering. What the writer remembers or forgets usually (but not always, such as in the case of trauma) mirrors the writer's sense of what is meaningful. Therefore, remembering involves a process that also implies forgetting. This selective process is applied not only in creating a life narrative but also extends to larger historical narratives that fashion cultural memory. De Certeau (1988) postulates that historians are not immune from this process because they begin with "the pieces that the imagination of their society has organized beforehand" (1988, 288), and write from within their cultural framework of values. National identities are formed through historical narrations that suppress "the unthinkable[1] in order for a new identity to *become* thinkable" (de Certeau's emphasis 1988, 4). In spite of the suppression of all that "this new understanding of the past holds to be irrelevant," fragments persist that de Certeau compares to "shards" which represent "remainders left aside by an explication" (1988, 4). These suppressed stories represent "'resistances,' 'survivals,' or delays [that] discreetly perturb … a system of interpretation" (de Certeau 1988, 4) such as those which more official narratives have sought to impose. Such historical narratives have played a role in oppressions. Traveller historical narratives represent an alternative "system of interpretation" that contests the univocality of official versions of history.

In the case of Travellers, popular belief held (and academic treatises sometimes concurred) that Travellers were "descendants of peasants forced into landlessness and mobility by the evictions and famines suffered by the Irish during the centuries of British domination" (Helleiner 2000, 30). Although these theories are lacking in historical evidence, they have shaped popular imagination as well as government policy. Helleiner (2000) observes that this perception of Traveller origins shaped official policies in the 1960s when "a state settlement program … was promoted as the action of a benevolent state motivated by a national duty to 're-settle' victims of colonialism" (2000, 30). Traveller oral histories contest this reading of history.

That Travellers rewrite historical narratives dominated by others asserts their need to address their present circumstances as reverberations of the past. If one accepts Luke Gibbons' (1996) argument that Irish history is "an open-ended narrative" (1996, 158), no single interpretation can be considered definitive. Gibbons asserts "[t]he impossibility of gaining direct access to the past … because it is part of an unresolved historical process which engulfs the present. It is lived history" (1996, 157). Certainly, pre-history (i.e., pre-literate history) is not inscribed and therefore cannot be a reified text. Moreover, the bias of official histories tends to ignore the "small" stories of ordinary citizens and valorizes the

[1] The "unthinkable" would be those narratives that are considered inconceivable since they contradict established beliefs. For example, Japanese historians prefer to ignore much of the evidence that Japan was an expansionist, aggressor nation prior to and during World War II, and instead reaffirm narratives of victimization. This is an extreme example of the manner whereby nation-states create historical narratives and is used to illustrate what de Certeau probably means by the term, "unthinkable", i.e., an idea that is so repugnant to the moral sensibilities of a group (like a nation) that it must be wholly rejected. The unthinkable thus becomes an idea which must be suppressed.

"big" events of the public domain, the military and political struggles. Such an emphasis has tended to preclude female activity from the narrative of history, as well as excluding the stories of lower social classes as insignificant. In this way, dominant narratives reproduce existing inequalities.

Dominant ideologies create the categories of representation while people excluded from public discourse experience these categories in ways that often diverge radically from more official representations (Stone-Mediatore 2003, 180). In Maher (1998), an old-time Traveller nicknamed the doll-man[2] verifies these areas of neglect when he remarks that gaps in representation exclude Traveller experience: "'The written history is very warped in its composition and truth'" (Maher 1998, 105). By identifying "*written*" history as problematic, he infers the existence of alternative, oral histories. In the same exchange, Maher argues the merits of formal education for Travellers, even as he recognizes his education as an incomplete perspective because all references to Travellers within the nation were erased. In response to this omission, Maher moves towards a partial validation of oral representations when he adds: "'Remembering, too, the many great old storytellers I have known and listened to on the road as a boy, I can easily overlook the truth of the official written history of Ireland'" (1998, 157). Although maintaining official history as a version of the "truth", Maher nevertheless suggests that Traveller stories perform an important symbolic function, history as interpretive narrative which will be discussed below.

Maher's remark suggests that there is a rationale by which truth status is assigned to some versions of history, a process of selection and interpretation that produces "a 'régime' of truth" (Foucault 1980, 133). Such regimes of truth, whether sanctioned through secular or religious institutions, tend to silence alternative versions but these latter narratives continue to proliferate among more marginalized groups who in their turn may dismiss official versions of history. Traveller retellings of apocryphal stories of the pre-historic origins of Ireland challenge the way "historical weight is differently accorded to different accounts, some of which become included in official history, [while] others [are] relegated to memory" (Cruikshank 2005, 6). Oral history represents a knowledge base that until recently, tended to be dismissed as "inadequate" under the literate criteria of Western law and academe[3], considered unable to

[2] The doll-man gets his nickname from his métier as an ambulatory performer who presents marionette shows.

[3] The Canadian legal precedent described at the end of Part II of this volume illustrates how this is changing.

measure up to standards of historicity that ascribed more authority to written documentation as the most reliable authentication of fact[4]. John Locke's *An Essay Concerning Human Understanding* exemplifies this emphasis where "the *written* text enjoys the status of an originating presence, and is the standard against which the inferior claims to truth of speech and tradition may be judged" (italics in Gibbons 1996, 153). Facing colonial discourses that justified colonization in the absence of "civilization", Gibbons (1996) asserts that "native Irish historians" advanced an Irish antiquity that was "culturally inscribed" (1996, 153) to counter colonialist expansionism. However, their proposals of an ancient, sophisticated civilization in pre-conquest Ireland "depended to a large extent on an oral heritage, and thus had to contend with a prejudice *against* popular memory" (italics in Gibbons 1996, 153). Travellers, speaking and writing against neo-colonial scripts, face a similar prejudice regarding the legitimacy of their oral histories. Indeed, even to label Traveller stories as "appropriations", "rewritings" or "retellings" of mainstream accounts accords more authenticity to the latter, for such phrasing implies that Traveller stories are merely reworking established conventions and discourses and that the migration of ideas and symbols and narratives only occurs in one direction. (The erroneousness of this assumption will be further explored in Part III.) Traveller stories rearticulate various well-known versions of Irish pre-history, thereby challenging the hegemony of these accounts through diversity but at the same time, the oral basis of their renderings face the same challenges regarding their legitimacy as many earlier Irish historians did.

Before proceeding to a discussion of the various Traveller narratives, some of the features as relating to various definitions of Irishness will be explored, since these represent the frameworks of national identity within which Travellers must speak. After centuries of British domination, the rhetoric on both sides of the political and geographical divide has supposed the existence of various inherent, fundamental differences between the British and Irish peoples, dividing practices which have served political objectives. As noted above, the British frequently used the rhetoric of inferiority to justify colonization as a benign and "civilizing" influence. Prolonged efforts on the part of the Irish people to achieve self-

---

[4] While written accounts certainly carry authority; pictorial, decorative, ceremonial and functional artifacts, as well as archaeological sites are also very useful to extrapolate information about pre-literate cultures. Of course, these are interpreted in accordance with certain biases and assumptions already held by the scholarly community, paradigms which may take time to reorient in the light of new or contradictory evidence.

rule sometimes erupted in armed struggle; Irish independence was also frequently fought for within the intellectual and political arenas, employing rhetoric which outlined competing claims. In the first decades of the 20th century, popular Irish views characterize Englishness as the very antithesis of Irishness, especially as relating to moral issues[5]. Perceived differences were based on economic organization, religion, and moral fibre. These widespread stereotypes could be summarized as national caricatures: if the British were licentious Protestant shopkeepers, the Irish were pious Catholic farmers. The doll-man, a Traveller character in Maher's autobiography (1998), identifies the ills of Ireland as "class-consciousness", a conclusion that also coincides with Joyce's analysis. He attributes "greed, ambition and pride" to "the influx of foreigners" (1998, 106), a reference that, given the time frame – the first half of the 20th century – alludes to the English colonial regime. This attribution of social ills to a former colonial power indicates the unresolved after-effects of colonization still resonant in the Irish psyche.

According to Gibbons (1996), one frequent defence mechanism employed against disparaging colonial discourse was to create a "coherent narrative form on the amorphous mass of Irish history" (1996, 155). Gibbons' contention (1996) concurs with de Certeau's conclusions (1988) identifying the historical narrative as a text that "has eliminated otherness and its dangers in order to retain only those fragments of the past which are locked into the puzzle of a present time" (1988, 287). Accordingly, Gibbons (1996) considers the history of Ireland to be a much more diverse and fragmented construct than Irish nationalist historians had previously acknowledged for fear of reinforcing British stereotypes. Noting the degree to which such histories racialized the Irish and how succinctly these unifying myths correlated with eighteenth-century beliefs concerning "primitivism" and the so-called "benevolent colonialism of Matthew Arnold" (1996, 156), Gibbons (1996) argues that Irish nationalist "re-inventions" of a glorious Celtic past are, in reality, "an extension of colonialism rather than a repudiation of it" (1996, 156).

In Joyce's (oral) genealogy, references to her family's intermarriage with "travellers from other countries" (2000, 1), including Spanish ancestors and a grandmother with a "Norman" name (2000, 1) as descended from "English travellers" (2000, 1), reflects the centuries of European influence in Ireland. Her embracing of diversity functions to counter those nationalistic discourses which stress cultural isolation and

[5] Moral distinctions paralleled to a certain degree in Traveller writing where non-Travellers are depicted as the "other" (see Hayes 2006).

racial purity, i.e., those narratives which would deny or downplay the effects of centuries of intercultural exchange in Irish society's development. More importantly, however, Joyce's insistence on an ancient Irish lineage which places the Traveller presence in Ireland in the pre-colonial era contradicts the unsubstantiated yet widely-held claim that the Traveller community are the descendants of Irish peasants displaced by the Famine (Helleiner 2000, 30). Once again, Joyce (2000) highlights the intergenerational transmission of knowledge in oral cultures, and indicates her trust in that same process when she states: "there's a lot of history behind [Travellers] though there's not much written down – it's what you get from your grandfather and what he got from his grandfather" (2000, 1). Although she begins by acknowledging that some of her ancestors "went on the road in the Famine", she emphasizes that "more of them have been travelling for hundreds of years", and traces their presence in Ireland to "St Patrick's time" (2000, 1). Her reference to other ancestors "burned out during the Cromwell evictions" (2000, 2) in the seventeenth century highlights another seminal episode in Ireland's tragic past. The orally-transmitted genealogy of her own family illustrates how family histories frequently incorporate historical events as milestones in the collective memory. Joyce cleverly uses these historical events as touchstones which resonate in a particular way with the reader who has a knowledge of Irish history. Whether non-Traveller or Traveller, the Irish people remember and commemorate these milestones in certain, specific ways. Republicans have tended to consider[6] the Cromwellian evictions, for example, as a particularly poignant example of the brutality of colonialism. Joyce uses these collective narratives to foster a sense of shared history, at the same time as she differentiates between the Traveller and "settled" cultures. For example, she asserts that the flexibility of nomadism made Travellers "used to coping with cold and hardship and hunger, they could survive anywhere because they had their own way of working and their own culture" (2000, 2), and concludes that because of their greater survival skills, some of the evictees "married in with travellers" during the time of the Cromwellian evictions.

---

[6] In the past three decades or so, revisionist historians have either tried to refute these widely-held beliefs or at least to nuance their presumed negativity. See Kennedy's (1996) critical work on the concept of historical Irish "folk-traumas" (1996, 186), i.e., he typifies those historical views that emphasize British colonialism as particularly harmful as grossly exaggerated in the "Out of History: Ireland, that 'Most Distressful Country'" chapter (1996, 185-223) published in *Colonialism, Religion and Nationalism in Ireland.*

While homogenous versions of Irish history were helpful for the nationalist cause precisely because of the unifying power of such mythologies, Gibbons (1996) is astute in noting that they were sometimes of a fabricated nature. Drawing its members from the Protestant Anglo-Irish Ascendancy as the Literary Revival did, it was in the interests of this privileged minority, originally of British extraction but with certain Irish loyalties and nationalist sentiments, to create a "supra-historical", pre-Christian narrative of Irishness inspired by Celtic mythologies that would allow for more inclusive definitions of Irish belonging. At the same time, tales of a glorious past offered an inspirational counterweight to the historical inequalities suffered under colonialism, their inferior social standing and the centuries-long absence of political power for the Irish within their own country.

While the Celtic Revival's emphasis on nationalism as a cultural movement was intended to circumvent the potentially-difficult consequences the Protestant minority faced if national belonging became defined by religious affiliation, this is exactly what happened in post-independence Ireland. Bourke (1995, 1996) outlines the tendency to conflate Irishness and Catholicism in the post-famine years of the 19th century and is harsh in her assessment of the consequences of this socio-cultural construction. She traces the growing influence of the Catholic Church in the early 20th century to a spirit of collusion within "the propertied middle class [who] dictated a repressive social morality based on a newly centralized, authoritarian, and misogynist Catholicism" (Bourke 1995, 4). The social cohesion achieved by the pressures to conform to rigid standards of moral behaviour effectively silenced any dissenting voices that might have represented difference. Travellers, who by and large are Catholic, were subsumed into this Irish homogeneity by virtue of being almost completely undifferentiated within the national discourse – except as the occasional object of study with the goal of "re-integrating" them into society. Although Travellers experienced the effects of these assimilationist policies as detrimental, the government interpreted their actions as the righting of old "wrongs". While on the one hand "anti-camping" laws prohibited "illegal" camping, Travellers and Traveller advocates witnessed successive governments fail to deliver on promises to provide "official" sites, despite much lobbying on the part of Traveller and other minority rights activists.

Metaphorically speaking, Nan Joyce's autobiography can be viewed as an attempt to write Travellers into the nation where belonging is conceived of as an "imagined" space. Her community's daily struggles with repressive settlement policies – forced evictions – mean that a good deal of her autobiography focuses on the "day-to-day" struggle for space within the physical contours of a nation. Joyce's citing[7] of MacColl's didactic poem / song "The Moving-on Song" epitomizes one of the major preoccupations of her autobiography, i.e., national belonging as an actual struggle to find physical space and personal security. The poem highlights the policy of forced evictions as **a** reprehensible one that is motivated by bigotry and intolerance for the most part. The verses of this poem are interspersed over a few pages of the autobiographical text that describes a campaign of police harassment her Traveller family experienced during one of their many stays in England.[8] Local police[9] would continually

---

[7] The decision to incorporate these poems into the body of the autobiographical text has been commented on by Delaney (2006) who writes that Joyce's incorporation of popular and traditional verses "attests to the significance of oral records" (2006, 33).

[8] As has been noted, borders between The Irish Republic, Northern Ireland, Scotland and England are / were frequently traversed as Traveller families followed employment opportunities, including seasonal labour. (Many "settled" Irish also travelled to England during the same period, sometimes for temporary work, but sometimes settling more permanently.) It is interesting to note that in no way did residency outside of Ireland diminish Joyce's claim to Irishness. As she explains, "The travellers are peculiar people, although they were never really wanted in Ireland, they were outcasts in their own country still they had great love for it. When they were away the first place they would sing about was Ireland. No matter where they'd be it was always Irish songs and 'God bless Ireland' when they'd great drunk" (2000, 24). Elsewhere, in *Moving Stories: Traveller Women Write* (1992), a collection of short autobiographies of "Irish Travelling women who have been in Southwark [England] for the last five years" (Gaffey 1992, 8), Kathleen McDonagh clarifies her ethnicity more succinctly, "I am Irish but I was born in Manchester in June 1965" (McDonagh 1992, 49). This suggests that for Travellers living in England, their place of birth has less meaning than their cultural heritage.

[9] Although this particular incident occurred while they were in England, it represents only one incident in a similar pattern of harassment across both England and Ireland. In fact, the two countries differed little in terms of anti-camping policies and their implementation through constant police harassment. However, Nan Joyce's sister, Chrissie Ward, claims that the police in Northern Ireland were worse in their abuse because Irish Travellers are predominantly Catholic and the police were predominantly Protestant. In her autobiography (conducted as an interview) in *Traveller Ways, Travellers Words* (1992), Ward testifies to the anti-Catholic slurs of the police when she quotes them as saying, "'Ye dirty Fenians. Go on ye pack o' Fenians. Ye should be up on your own country. Yiz are not welcome down here" (Ward 1992, 48), as they drove the Travellers from their tents. Similarly, religious differences seem to have prompted Joyce to return to

uproot them throughout the course of the day so that they were constantly moving from one area to another. "The police would say, 'Move on, move on'"(2000, 75), a statement which echoes the penultimate line repeated in each of the six stanzas of the poem[10]. The first two lines of the poem recall

---

Ireland from England on more than one occasion (such as the time a doctor in an English hospital suggested she practice artificial birth control).

[10] Ewan MacColl's "The Moving-on Song", interspersed in the text of *My Life on the Road* appears below. (Another verse appears on page 29 which will not be looked at.) Because the stanzas are separated in the text, line numeration will be limited to the page where stanzas appear, then begin again at line one, etc., on subsequent pages:

> Once you could pull in your caravan
> To a sheltered spinney or to open ground
> But the law moved in with the barbed-wired fence
> And they said that your camp was a prime offence
> And told you to shift and keep on going
> And move along, get along, move along, get along,
> Go: move: shift.
>
> Born in the middle of the afternoon
> In a horse-drawn trailer on the old A5
> The big twelve-wheeler shook my bed
> 'You can't stop here', the policeman said
> 'You'd better get born in some place else,
> So move along, get along, move along, get along,
> Go: move: shift.'
>
> Born in the tattie lifting-time
> In an old bow tent near a tattie field
> The farmer said 'The work's all done,
> It's time that you was moving on
> You'd better get born in some place else,
> So move along, get along, move along, get along,
> Go: move: shift.'
>
> Born on a common near a building site
> Where the ground was rutted with the trailer's wheels
> The local people said to me
> 'You'll lower the price of property,
> You'd better get born in some place else,
> So move along, get along, move along, get along,
> Go: move: shift.'

a more tolerant past when, "Once you could pull in with your caravan / To a sheltered spinney or to open ground" (2000, 75: 1-2). The sense of a safe haven connoted by "sheltered spinney", and the more informal use of space suggested by "open ground" contrast with the present rigorous application of "the law" in the next line that hints at the state-sponsored suppression of nomadism:

> But the law moved in with the barbed-wire fence
> And they said that your camp was a prime offence
> And told you to shift and keep on going
> And move along, get along, move along, get along,
> Go: move: shift. (2000, 75: 3-7)

The irony of "prime offence" suggests that repressive tactics on the part of the state far outweigh the "crime" of nomadism. The allusion to "barbed-wire" evokes internment camps, concentration camps or prisons, and emphasizes confinement motifs, including containment and loss of freedom. The imagery here highlights the prejudice that motivates the faceless individual who is representative of state-sponsored authority. Each of the stanzas wherein quotation marks indicate speech, these

---

> Wagon, tent or trailer-born
> Last week, last year, or in far-off days
> Born here or afar, seven miles away
> There's always men nearby who'll say
> 'You'd better get born in some place else,
> So move along, get along, move along, get along,
> Go: move: shift.'
>
> The winter sky was hung with stars
> And one shone brighter than the rest
> The Wise Men came so stern and strict
> And brought the order to evict
> 'You'd better get born in some place else
> So move along, get along, move along, get along,
> Go: move: shift.'
>
> Once you could settle for a week or two
> On a public common or a riverside
> But the council chased us off the sites
> And they said 'You people have no rights
> You'd better get moving some place else
> So move along, get along, move along, get along,
> Go: move: shift.' (Joyce 2000, 75, 77, 80, 85)

authority figures are portrayed as cold and unfeeling individuals who remove the Traveller presence in their vicinity without heed to the consequences of their actions on Traveller lives. That economic interests are also a driving factor in this ongoing harassment is underlined in the next stanza: "The local people said to me / 'You'll lower the price of property'" (2000, 77: 17-18). Joyce's awareness that class is an important factor in their persecution substantiates Sibley's (1995) contention that economic interests often buttress more "modern" forms of persecution. Sibley (1995) describes the "eviction … of many English[11] Gypsy sites," and the persecution which such minorities face in economic terms and "demonstrate[s] the need of the state to secure the interests of capital through socio-spatial control of 'deviance' and cultural difference" (1995, 84). Joyce (2000) too, testifies to the economic justifications which underlie many evictions. When her family were evicted from a roadside early one morning, they tried to pull in next to some "swanky-looking houses … with a big high wall round them" (2000, 93) to make something to eat. However, "[t]he very minute we pulled in a gang of people came out from the houses. They were calling us names and shouting, 'You're not camping here!'" (2000, 93). Socio-economic spatial divisions, including the widespread practice of developing suburban neighbourhoods by income segregation typical of much modern urban planning have the effect of further isolating certain segments of society so that there is no chance whatsoever for dialogue and mutual understanding between different social and cultural groups.

Joyce (2000) highlights the manner whereby the control of space is actually an outward manifestation of conflicting power relations. In MacColl's "The Moving-on Song" that she cites, Travellers are relegated to the borderlands, both figurative and actual. In the first of the four stanzas that open chapter nine, Traveller babies are described as born on

---

[11] Citing remarks and studies of "English Gypsies" can sometimes be appropriate for several reasons. First, the permeability of borders means that these nomadic groups not only encounter each other, but also sometimes live in close vicinity. Joyce recalls one encounter from her childhood when they camped with "Romany gypsies" (Joyce 2000, 23). That her father learned their language and they learned his again indicates that even endogamous cultures intermingle and even sometimes intermarry, as Joyce again verifies. Secondly, both groups share a traditional nomadic lifestyle and anthropological studies such as Okely's find many of the same customs and taboos. Whether English or Irish Traveller, or English Gypsy (or Roma), all face similar housing and mobility "issues". Finally, all nomadic people living in Europe suffer persecution and discrimination. This is not to say that a "cultural transference" is applicable in every case, but that it sometimes can be.

the roadside: "Born in the middle of the afternoon / In a horse-drawn trailer on the old A5 / The big twelve-wheeler shook my bed" (2000, 77: 1-3). The first line in the third of these four stanzas, "Born on a common near a building site" (2000, 77: 15), expresses the liminality of the Traveller community's social position in terms of the nation's landscape. Their inability to find a figurative space within the nation translates to inhabiting the actual physical periphery of society, camped on the edges of towns, larger urban centres and abandoned industrial areas. Their physical segregation is a tangible and poignant motif for the marginalized status Travellers occupy in Irish society.

Joyce uses this didactic poem in order to highlight the reality of social issues. By doing so, she maintains the traditional rhetorical functions of lyric poetry, and rediscovers a more public forum for poetry. Incorporating the conventions of the "traditional" poetic form, i.e., versification, rhyme and repetition (the latter two elements retained as memory aids from the time when poetry was an oral performance), Joyce effectively argues the case against forced evictions, assimilation, and the absence of a Traveller "space" within the "construct" that is the nation. Historically, the gradual evolution of poetry away from spoken recitations to an increased emphasis on literary forms was reflected in a simultaneous shift of focus from the outward concerns of the social world and the spoken word, to the more inward, self-reflexivity and subjectivity of the lyric poem[12]. Joyce's use of poetry for "political" purposes parallels the tendency in her autobiography to downplay a more self-absorbed subjectivity and emphasize the more comprehensive and community-oriented concerns.

Because Travellers have been "written out" of history, Joyce attempts to establish Travellers as "patriots" and asserts their active participation in the forging of the modern Irish nation. Her apocryphal story of gun smuggling by Travellers during the "troubles"[13] challenges Travellers'

---

[12] The lyric poem became strongly associated with Romanticism, the individuated self and the literary. Ong (1991) identifies the "Romantic Movement" as "the beginning of the end of the … oral art form" (1991, 158). Ong includes the epic poem as one example of an orally-influenced genre that is no longer produced as a viable contemporary form.

[13] "Troubles" was a euphemism for the sectarian violence that erupted in the late 60s and continued until the signing of the Good Friday Accord, April 10, 1998. Here though, as Joyce's reference to the "old IRA" indicates "troubles" refers to the civil war that ignited shortly after the signing of the Anglo-Irish Treaty which split the country, granting 26 counties dominion status, the "Irish Free State", but partitioning the six predominantly Protestant, Ulster counties in the North (Pašeta 2003, 83-4).

"victimhood" status and depicts them as active agents in the nation's development. This humorous anecdote was related to her father by the Traveller couple involved. The story goes that the Black and Tans[14], the "auxiliaries" active during the Irish War of Independence (1919 – 1921), a group who were notorious for their brutality, were about to search the Traveller couple's cart where guns were hidden when the husband, who was walking beside the cart, whispered to his wife, seated in the cart, "'Scratch' … so she started scratching. He walked over to the two soldiers, scratching away, and he said to them 'Have you got any cure for lice, sir? I'm walking alive.' When the Black and Tans heard this they backed away … and … wouldn't go near the cart" (2000, 27). The humour lies in the shrewd manipulation of the soldiers' prejudices and fear of the "other", prejudgments which make them appear ridiculous. Because thc Traveller couple turn negative stereotypes to their favour, the story operates almost as a "trickster" motif where the wily trickster or anti-hero outwits the Black and Tans who are a byword for foreign occupation and the brutality of colonisation in Ireland. The trickster is a shapeshifter who has a talent for adapting to difficult circumstances. He / she is a creator god gifted with the ability to rise from the ashes of disaster. Therefore, the role of trickster is usually played by characters of "weaker" social status who use their intelligence and wit to achieve their goals. In addition to highlighting Travellers as agents of history, the story points to their loyalty as republicans and patriots, underlining Joyce's persistent argument: i.e., we are Travellers *and* we are Irish.

Cruikshank (1998, 2005) supports years of field research in northern Canada amongst First Nations elders and storytellers with the findings of anthropologists and historians. In her essay, "Oral Tradition and Oral History – Reviewing Some Issues" (2005), Cruikshank cites a study by Cohen who, when working amongst tribal clans in East Africa, noted the fact that those clans with superior economic resources were able to record their genealogies, histories which "came to be accorded considerable status and gradually assumed the character of official history" (2005, 4). Other tribes "whose histories were overlooked in the process … never accepted that the recorded accounts represented their interests, nor did the written versions assume any particular authority in their eyes" (2005, 4). Cohen's findings are of interest in the context of this discussion not only because they mirror attitudes to official discourse as expressed in Maher's

[14] Experiencing low recruitment, the Black and Tans were recruited into the Royal Irish Constabulary from the mainly unemployed veterans of World War I. Trench warfare was not adequate training and they were said to act "as an occupation army" (McCormack 1986).

memoir, but also because of the degree to which they can parallel transformations in the history of a country such as Ireland when the early Irish monks first transcribed pre-Christian myths. Early monks appropriated by Christianizing Celtic customs, myths and beliefs, reifying these Christianized versions through the act of inscription[15].

Gibbons (1996) has argued that subsequent to the Williamite defeat at the Battle of the Boyne in 1690, it became even more crucial for wounded Catholic aspirations to advance positive counter-discourses in order to dilute the inferiorizing rhetoric of the British colonizers. As discussed above, it was "in the interests of native Irish historians" to resist the nature / culture dualism that permitted the legitimization of colonial occupation in other British colonies by allocating the colonised / appropriated land to the emptiness of "nature". Unsurprisingly therefore, previous generations of Irish historians promoted the idea of a Celtic cultural continuity in Ireland "from the dawn of antiquity" onwards (Gibbons 1996, 153). At their most essential, Traveller narratives propose a similar approach and for quite similar reasons, i.e., in order to counteract non-Traveller beliefs that place Traveller origins in a narrative of defeat, as victims of the Famine, which denies them status as an enduring and separate culture.

The possibility that Traveller versions of "apocryphal" Irish history have any substantive historical basis – i.e., that they may be as "true", or as "false" (in the sense of oversimplified and unsubstantiated) – as more "official" versions – which are also based on very meagre historical "evidence", is an assessment of Traveller self-representations / narratives that all scholars do not acquiesce with, e.g., Lanters, 2005. While Lanters (2005) recognizes the positive symbolic value of such narratives, her assessments that "Travellers sometimes endow themselves with

---

[15] Because oral tradition precedes written documentation, the facts of prehistory are much more difficult to ascertain, and archaeological texts permit even more latitude for conjecture than historical texts. Scholar R.P.C. Hanson (1989) points out that while very little is known *in fact* about St. Patrick (other than his British origins), much of that which is accepted as apocryphal wisdom is in his regard actually not true. Hanson asserts, "He did not banish snakes from Ireland. He did not illustrate the doctrine of the Trinity by the example of the shamrock ..." (Hanson 1989, 24), etc. Today, all that remains of Patrick's written communications are the *Letter to Coroticus* and the *Confession* (Hanson 1989, 23) (with a third work, *St. Patrick's Breastplate*, ascribed to him by tradition but, at least in its written form, traced to three centuries after his death (O'Donoghue 1989, 45)). The earliest books about his life were penned about two hundred years after his death and were therefore based on oral sources. The absence of definitive sources and evidence has not lessened the enduring influence and symbolic value of these apocryphal legends in the shaping of Irish identity.

respectable ancestors" and that "historical self-explanation often takes the form of poetic self-invention" (2005, 28), suggests that she regards any truth substance in Traveller oral histories as implausible[16]. Stone-Mediatore (2003) usurps this reification of the written text over other types of evidence when she proposes that one should read "the historical text as a story" (2003, 165). Rather than dismiss oral accounts completely, the researcher who takes due account of popular belief opens the investigative mind to alternative interpretations of the historical and archaeological evidence. Maher's mother underlines the educative importance of these "apocryphal" accounts and stresses the reliability of the speakers when she says, "'We on the road can't write our deeds, but we do remember them and pass them down faithfully by word of mouth'" (1998, 68). Maher appreciates the merit of both types of "knowledge", therefore. Although he received only four years of formal education, this was a thorough one which gave him a good basis in Irish literature and history. To this conventional canon, he brought his "insider" knowledge of traditional Traveller songs and stories. Nevertheless, he noticed discrepancies and questioned why the stories he heard at school were "different" from those he heard at home. In a conversation with one of his tutors, he brings up St. Patrick. "'You never tell about him being a traveller,'" he says (Maher 1998, 127). The Brother initially casts doubt on this unfamiliar adaptation. "'[Y]ou may have heard a false version'", he answers, but young Seán objects, "'No, it was not false, it's the one in the schoolbook that's wrong'" (Maher 1998, 127). The Brother then concedes that there are, in fact, many versions of history, each of them with a different view of events: "'With Irish history, English, Danish and what have you, perhaps yours is not false, after all'"(Maher 1998, 127).

Although the Brother's first reaction may have been to dismiss Seán's version, oral history scholars increasingly recognize similarities between both written and oral accounts. As Cruikshank (1998, 2005) argues: "All are structured, interpretive, combative, and subjective as well as objective" (2005, 3). Instead of casting doubt on orality as a less reliable approach than that pertaining to more "authentic" historical documents, historian Judith Binney characterizes all history as a form of storytelling, discovery and the uncovering of "truths" that are constructed during the time and context in which the interpretation is being written / rewritten: "'All histories derive from a particular time, a particular place and a particular

[16] In this regard, Lanters (2005) can be seen to reflect the views of British empirical philosophers such as John Locke and David Hume, both of whom rejected oral representations based on "popular memory" (Gibbons 1996, 154) as too removed from the reliability of the printed text.

cultural heritage'" (Binney cited in Cruikshank 2005, 3). Binney also contests the claim that oral histories are less reliable because they change over time, and notes that "Eurohistory … has a lifespan of about ten or fifteen years before it gets reinterpreted; in contrast the life of an oral history is considerably longer" (Binney cited in Cruikshank 2005, 4). Here, Binney is referring not to literal "facts", but to the interpretation of the data which the historiographer sources in the attempt to bridge the gap between the writing present and an irretrievable past. As Bakhtin (1895-1975) remarked, "It is impossible to change the factual, thing-like side of the past, but the meaningful, expressive, speaking side can be changed, for it is unfinalized" (Bakhtin cited in Gibbons 1996, 3). Since the meanings ascribed to the past change according to the political climate and ideological stance of the writing "present", there exists no body of pristine historical data that can claim exclusive monopoly on the description of the truth.

Assumptions regarding the inherent inferiority of oral forms of knowledge – as commonly held within literate cultures today – fail to address the manner whereby the mechanisms of power legitimate some stories over others. While St. Patrick, St. Brigid and St. Kevin all are accepted as "founding figures" within Irish national discourse, how to interpret these largely mythical figures and decipher historical fact – as based on physical evidence – from legend, is by no means an easy and uncontroversial process. As Michel de Certeau (1988) concludes, "'[h]istorical facts' … speak of 'choices' which are precedents, and which are therefore not the result of observation — which are not even verifiable but … only 'falsifiable'" (de Certeau citing Popper 1988, 59). It is also important to note that scholarly paradigms and discourses can change over time. Feminist scholars, for example, have interpreted historical artifacts such as rock engravings to support the argument that Brigid was first revered as an Irish goddess[17] prior to being venerated as a saint by the then newly-fledged Christian faith in Ireland. In the absence of adequate historical documentation, Traveller versions of early Irish history are as difficult to prove or discount as are the varying interpretations of Celtic legends. Traveller "reappropriations" of foundational myths are driven by motives which are not dissimilar to the Anglo-Irish Literary Revival's emphasis on traditional stories and legends: firstly as a positive reflection of self-identity, especially important as a response to negative interpellations, and secondly, as a way of writing a "space" or a "place of

[17] Mary Condren's argument in *The Serpent and the Goddess: Women, Religion and Power in Celtic Ireland*. (1989, 48-78).

belonging" within the fabric of the nation. The first impetus is largely an interiorised and affirmative narrative of the self while the second is turned outwards so as to engage in a more public discourse.

Cruikshank (1998, 2005) has detailed the symbolic function which such stories serve as positive self-narrative after having worked with First Nations women elders in the Canadian Yukon. Cruikshank (1998) noticed that these women incorporated traditional stories into their lives in ways that helped them in "evaluating contemporary choices", and concluded that "If one has optimistic stories about the past … one can draw on internal resources to survive and make sense of arbitrary forces that might otherwise seem overwhelming" (Cruikshank 1998, xii). Adaptability is a noteworthy feature of these "traditional" stories. Traveller stories that recast Traveller characters in positive and pivotal roles in nation-building fulfill this same helpful self-constructing and self-actualizing role. The significance of the symbolic in this process has been cited by Lanters (2005) who refers to "writing one's life story [as] taking control of one's own narrative, inventing oneself poetically, and imagining oneself into the future" (2005, 41)[18].

Maher (1998), like Joyce (2000), traces Irish Travellers back to at least St. Patrick's era, and asserts a Traveller presence in Ireland contiguous with the period when this Irish saint was evangelizing and Christianizing the island. His mother depicts an active Traveller participation in Patrick's ministry. Her version of the traditional St. Patrick's story contrasts with the one gleaned from Gaelic speakers in the West of Ireland as recorded by Lady Gregory in her *A Book of Saints and Wonders*, published in 1906. The latter account correlates with the Traveller "version" in that both locate a Traveller presence in Ireland as contemporaneous with St. Patrick's ministry. In Lady Gregory's rendition of this traditional Irish folktale, St. Patrick curses the "tinkers" for trying to deceive him for their own personal gain. Patrick's curse, "[A]s for the tinkers, every man's face is against them and their face is against every man, and they get no ease or rest, but are ever and always travelling the world" (Gregory 1971, 44), "justifies" the persecution of Travellers as a "divine judgement" originating in their own nefarious nature. Helleiner (2000) notes that Traveller versions of these tales invert these traditional stories in which nomadism (whether Traveller or Roma or "Wandering Jew") is believed to be a punishment for deicide or the participation in the death of Christ. In Maher's mother's story of St. Patrick, not only do the Travellers offer the

---

[18] Maher's mother subverts this optimism somewhat by imagining the "future" as apocalyptic. The significance of this particular trope is discussed in Part III of this volume.

slave boy hospitality and refuge, thereby helping him escape his bondage, but also when he returns from mainland Europe years later, "'it was to [Travellers] that he first preached the words of Christ'" (Maher 1998, 70). This claim, suggesting that Travellers are a "chosen people" is also implied by her assertion that the Travellers "'became his disciples'" (1998, 70), a story that parallels the Biblical scene where Christ chooses ordinary fishermen to be his followers.[19]

Although Maher the writer is recording Traveller stories in his memoir, he almost invariably places the story in the mouth of the character associated with the story, which may be in deference to a sense of ownership of the story. It also may be due to the manner whereby Maher's memory functions, given that memory tends to have a spatial rather than a temporal context. That "this is especially true of childhood memories" (1991, 229) is also highlighted by Casey (1991). The boy Seán remembers his mother recounting the story of St. Patrick at bedtime as they waited for his father to return to their camp from the pub. The dread of his father's imminent arrival shows in his mother's fretting, "as soon as you hear him coming, scoot off into bed'" (1998, 69), so that for the reader – as most likely for Maher – the story is etched in a particular time and place and has particular associations. Such associations create a poignant dissonance between the story's mythic setting and the family's actual situation.

When his mother tells him that it was the Travellers who helped St. Patrick escape from slavery, young Seán immediately questions the veracity of her account: "'Mammy, this might have been a made-up story'" (1998, 68). Maher's approach here is typical of the manner whereby storytellers anticipate and address opposition before it even arises, either by dissipating audience scepticism or by admitting to their own doubts (Bourke 1996, 10). His mother admits that the story might not be true but adds, "'I believe it,'" and then argues at length in support of the reliability of oral tradition. She reasons, "'I know that this and other stories are passed down from generation to generation among the travellers, and they are not people who add to tales themselves'" (Maher 1998, 68). This last point highlights the cultural integrity of the storyteller:

> 'You must remember that the records of deeds in the past are always passed down by word of mouth. From listening at campfires when stories are told, you will know what great attention is given to detail. I have heard a story at one camp-fire and maybe years later I have heard the same story at another, the important details still unchanged. You must remember

---

[19] This idea of Travellers as a chosen people recurs more potently in the story of St. Kevin, discussed in Part III of this volume.

that story-telling is our only means of communication with the past.' (Maher 1998, 68)

In this passage, Maher's mother has drawn upon the same processes which disseminated such ancient works as the *Iliad* and the *Pentateuch*, amongst other influential Western works in the era before these oral transmissions were ever first committed to writing. Maher's mother is correct in saying, "'the important details [are] still unchanged,'" yet in emphasizing the faithfulness of a story over time, she elides the skill of the storyteller. Each performance involves improvisational adaptations with embellishments or omissions responsive to the particular audience so that no two oral performances are alike (Ong 1991). Emphasis on word-for-word accuracy is an obsession based on the textual model and such strictures never apply in the same manner to performances that cannot return to a written text to confirm their accuracy (Ong 1991). While Maher (1998) cherishes the stories he recounts, his insider / outsider status ensures an ambivalent feeling permeates his discussion of these issues. It is as if Maher is always stepping back and viewing these questions from the vantage point of somebody who has had a number of years of formal education.

Such "poetic" inventions as the Traveller "version" of St. Patrick's ministry in Ireland (at the very least) provide creative and constructive alternatives to conventional discourse in addition to the many silences and gaps in that same discourse. They demonstrate Traveller writers grasp of the significant role which symbols play in the discourse of national belonging. It is the underlying lessons of his mother's "tradition" as opposed to its "literal" historicity which moves the boy not only to dream, but (also) to defend those dreams. Maher defends the "truth" of his community's and his mother's stories. As a boy, Seán would often be invited into people's homes as he did his "rounds", begging or selling from door-to-door, as was commonplace in Ireland then. In a conversation with a non-Traveller family who had invited him in to eat, Seán was laughed at when he told them he wanted to be a priest. "'[I]magine having a tinker priest'" (1998, 64) was the response to his statement. Seán utilises the "collective lore" that is the oral tradition of the Traveller community to remonstrate with those who mock him, however. "'I'm not a tinker, I'm a traveller, and our Blessed Lord himself was a traveller, ma'am … My mother … told us, and it's true too, that Our Lord used to travel around all the time'" (Maher 1998, 65). His ability to defend himself underlines the positive potential of such folk-history for a community's narratives of self-determination. The boy's trust in the authority of his mother's words demonstrates the important intergenerational component that is characteristic of oral culture. When these forms of communication cease –

as is the current pattern worldwide as minority cultures are exposed to the electronic mass media – the intergenerational chain is disrupted. The danger then arises that the next generation may lose a link with their cultural heritage. This underlines the importance of Traveller writing as an important repository of social and cultural history, as Traveller writers are themselves frequently consciously aware, a means of recording a past so that it will be preserved for future generations.

Maher's mother's view that it is the "spirit" rather than "the letter" which is preserved in the oral tradition corresponds with Kadar's (2005) approach to the difficulties encountered as regards oral cultures and communal memory – (specifically) the problem of recovering the almost-obliterated stories of the Romany (Gypsy) victims of the Nazi Holocaust. Faced with the quandary that very few Romany survivors have recorded their stories in "more conventional autobiographical genres", Kadar accepts that "traces or fragments of autobiographical telling must stand in for" (2005, 223) more complete histories. She also comes to the understanding that "[m]emory registers what it felt like, not exactly what it was like and that slippage from "historical fact" to individual feeling and yearning is crucial to remember in our work in Autobiographical Studies" (Kadar 2005, 224). Despite the dearth of written testimony, many "traces of story and memory" (Kadar 2005, 226), and songs composed in the concentration camps have survived, all of which connect with the human dimensions of the past and are not contained in the facts and statistics about the Holocaust.

Interestingly, the Canadian legal system has had to move towards acknowledging the fact that the legends and oral traditions of certain minorities do have a substantive basis within the legal system. This has occurred in at least one court case involving First Nations' tribal land claims. In a court case that they initially lost (a decision later overturned), hereditary chiefs of the Gitxsan[20] nation argued, " that the case before the Supreme Court [of British Columbia] should not depend on the literal accuracy of [their] histories. ... Oral tradition is more than literal history and should not be reduced to mere historical data, they argued, though it does provide evidence for scholars studying the past" (Cruikshank 1998, 64). The first judge dismissed their arguments, but the Supreme Court of Canada overturned his judgement on the grounds that "the trial judge erred by not taking into account oral histories of the natives presented to the court to establish their occupation and use of the land" (Matas et al. 2006,

[20] Also spelled Gitksan.

1). The latter judgement recognized oral tradition[21] as not untenable, thereby opening the door for similar judgements. Extrapolating from this, Traveller claims that their ancestors numbered among the *filidh* of ancient Ireland (ambulatory "scholars and keepers of the flame of tribal wisdom" (Flannery 1997, 15)), have not been proven. Neither have they been disproved however, and therefore, the debate should remain open.

By writing to create new perspectives on shared symbols Joyce and Maher reshape the historical Irish landscape. While the "mists of time" may shroud many unknown aspects of the Irish experience, certain contemporary facts are always evident. Firstly, some stories and historical interpretations are deemed authentic while others are discounted, particularly where they challenge the dominant discourses of the status quo. Secondly, Travellers demonstrate the ability to put forward responses to historical omissions and errors that – whether judged as creative imaginings or as having some basis in oral tradition – can yet provide "positive" models against which present hardships or inequalities can be offset. These types of mythmaking are (clearly) not dissimilar to the Irish Literary Revival's constructions of nationalism as both "cultural" and "pre-colonial", and like the Anglo-Irish constructions, they help circumvent divisive issues that might otherwise jeopardize a community's claims to legitimate citizenship.

Part III of this volume begins by examining the crucial influence of the oral tradition in shaping the worldview that informs Maher's mother's miracle stories and Joyce's religious concepts and symbols. The dollman's "anti-modernist" viewpoints provide a narrative background to the economic and social hardships which give rise to "apocalyptic" perspectives as expressed by Maher's "traumatized" characters. These "apocalyptic" motifs ensure that the national trauma of colonialism, the collective trauma as inflicted on Travellers, and Maher's personal trauma coalesce narratively in his autobiography and form the basis of the discussion in the next chapter. Joyce's response to personal trauma – her social activism – provides a counterpoint to this discussion.

---

[21] However, almost a decade later, the land claim still has not been settled and according to the Gitxsan Chiefs' Office website, "resource extraction and development has continued unabated in the Gitxsan territories while the aboriginal title court action and treaty negotiations are under way" ("Who We Are").

Part III

Rewriting the Modern: Countering "Anglo-Saxon Empiricism"

I am ready to go home
through an autumn evening.

Suddenly,
without any warning, I can see them.

They form slowly out of the twilight.
Their faces. Arms. Greatcoats. And tears.

They are holding maps.
But the pages are made of fading daylight.
Their tears, made of dusk, fall across the names.

Although they know by heart
every inch and twist of the river
which runs through this town, and their houses—
every aspect of the light their windows found—
they cannot find where they come from:

The river is still there.
But not their town.
The light is there. But not their moment in it.

Then they faded.
And the truth is I never saw them.

—"The Colonists", Eavan Boland 1998

Speaking Against "Anglo-Saxon Empiricism": The World as Cosmos

Simplistic scenarios regarding appropriation and cultural domination cannot account for the capacity of the creative imagination to subvert hegemonic scripts[1]. While the more "elitist" and academic culture operates within established institutional frameworks, present-day cultural trends (the proliferation of electronic media sites, for example) indicate the extent to which culture propagates "from below", i.e., from the "grassroots". Traveller writing affirms the inherent intelligence and creativity of thinking, feeling human beings, even if their social position is not one of societal privilege. Given the ever-present risk that oral accounts and traditions will be lost forever (when the performer / narrator dies), Maher spends much time / space recounting traditional stories, always as attributed to a particular storyteller. In order to preserve these stories, and the way of life they represent, Maher undertakes to create a written record, even though inscribing the oral tradition poses the problem that is the absent "spontaneity" of the storytelling performance. While spoken language is always fluid, written language becomes a more static object, as separated from the scribe (Ong 1991). Orality is a language of presence. It is a live performance, an action and not an object. This is the compromise that is necessitated by modernity. Maher (1998) structures his accounts so that the setting of the retelling, the circumstances of the event itself, the characteristics of the storyteller and the reactions of the audience etc. are all set before the reader. By these means, a sense of the theatrical "timing" that is orality remains.

Besides stories featuring visitations from departed souls ("ghost" stories) – many of these conveyed by visitors to their campfire – his mother's repertoire includes miracle stories, in addition to apocalyptic tales. All of these genres share a common characteristic as evident in the narrative structure of the stories, i.e., a kind of religious veneration for the incredible, the fantastic and the inexplicable, as based on a belief in the supernatural and an afterworld. Space constraints mean that it would be impossible in this volume to investigate, in detail, the functions of ghost stories in Maher's text, but his mother's stories of miraculous wells and her tales of the apocalypse will be examined. The shocking pessimism incorporated in Maher's apocalyptic "predictions" can best be understood as a reflection of a particular worldview, but also as the reaction to the long-term stress that is sustained social marginalization. Eliade (1959, 1967) notes that in apocalyptic literature "the end of the world is never absolute; it is always followed by the creation of a new, regenerated

[1] On the other hand, the proliferation of the mass media means the tendency towards the co-option of minority cultural expressions can prove to be highly profitable. "Authenticity" has a market value. Recent examples of appropriation of "street"-culture include using graffiti, skateboarding, piercing, tattooing etc., to sell products such as soft drinks and running shoes ("The Merchants of Cool", 2001).

world" (Eliade 1967, 243). In Maher's mother's primary apocalyptic story, however, this new world does *not* include the Travellers as a people.

Standing in opposition to Maher's (1998) fatalism, Joyce's (2000) mystical experiences, as recounted a full decade after Maher, inspire a more inclusive perspective that leads her on to a more expansive role as a community leader. Ong (1967, 1991) and Eliade (1959, 1967) see both worldviews, however distinct in their outward manifestations, as typical of the universe of the oral thinker where the natural world is perceived as a manifestation of an all-pervasive "life force". Whether this be interpreted as a spirit or god / God, this presence imbues the world with meaning. In fact, the outward world makes manifest this God / god / spirit, in much the same way as literate societies consider "God" to be expressed through the medium of a written text. In a sense, the world is a living text to be read, and interpreted, and animated by the spirit. Like the spoken word, this text is an active force, always in movement, always changing, and one must always remain open to the divine made manifest. Ong (1967, 1991) identifies the grounds for difference between this viewpoint and the modern scientific standpoint of thought as language, and the cognitive differences that exist between orality and literacy.

How we experience language shapes how we experience our world. Because of "the centering action of sound", the world of oral – aural cultures surrounds and envelopes us like sound (Ong 1991, 73). In this worldview, human beings share kinship with the non-human world, whereas in worldviews that emphasize the visual, the universe becomes distant and removed. The emphasis on the visual in literate societies produces a marked distinction between the human being and its environment, one that allows for objectification or "thingness", and thereby facilitates scientific enquiry. Sass (1997) summarizes this spatial and psychic alienation as typical of modernity, a "desacralization" of space as "initiated by Galilean and Newtonian science and grounded in Cartesian dualism whereby the external world is stripped of all magical, religious, value-laden, or anthropomorphic characteristics and is grasped by a purely calculative rationality" (1997, 205). Basing his conclusions on Heidegger (1889-1976), Sass argues that "the objectivist vision of modern science and technology" (1997, 205) allows for the exploitation of other life forms and the earth's resources because the natural world is perceived "in terms of an ordering that accords with human categories and needs" (Sass 1997, 205)[2].

[2] Sass notes that Heidegger considered "the objectivist vision of modern science and technology [as] essentially subjectivist" (Sass 1997, 205).

O'Donoghue (1989, 2001) politicizes these philosophical trends when he depicts "empiricism" as a "British" invention. He sees a clear philosophical opposition between "Celtic" worldviews and the "English" worldview and identifies the philosophical materialism of "empiricism" as a uniquely "Anglo-Saxon" invention (this despite the fact that the roots of empiricism can be traced to Aristotle). O'Donoghue's theorisation is redolent of a nationalism which tends to define British and Irish national characteristics as comprising generally oppositional features. O'Donoghue also views the philosophy of empiricism as one of failure when he observes that "nearly all the great philosophers outside the Anglo-Saxon tradition accept the reality of an intelligible or spiritual world [as] distinct from the material world" (2001, 26)[3].

O'Donoghue's (1989, 2001) contention that British empiricism represents an intellectual rift with certain earlier notions of reality finds support in Gibbons (1996) who uncovers textual evidence that indicates the grave suspicions held by British eighteenth and nineteenth century intellectuals toward contemporaneous Irish philosophical worldviews. Empiricist philosopher David Hume (1711-1776), for example, opposed the preponderance of orality in Ireland, a facet of Irish culture which he perceived as antithetical to rationality. Hume, writing about Ireland in 1796, "[argued] that tradition and popular memory were indistinguishable from credulity and superstition" (Hume cited in Gibbons 1996, 154). Certainly, Hume's views, linking popular culture, religion and orality, fall in line with the Enlightenment philosophy of his era, where "religion … retains a voice" through a connection to orality and popular culture, but "one which is superstitious, deprived of reason, and foreign to the knowledge already possessed by the enlightened milieus" (de Certeau 1988, 184). Furthermore, de Certeau (1988) argues, because "the group (or the individual) is legitimized", or defined, "by what it excludes" (1988, 5), by what it is *not*, "the rationality of the Enlightenment maintains a necessary relation with its other" (1988, 174). These civilizing, educating compulsions struggle to fill a lack in the unacceptable Other — that which de Certeau lists as the "illiterate populous, the child, the savage" (1988, 174). Hume meanwhile attributes the difficulty the English encountered in the "'subduing and civilizing of that country'" (Hume cited in Gibbons

[3] For the sake of clarity, the "empiricism" O'Donoghue (2001) refers to is assumed to be a type of materialistic positivism that underpins the scientific method, i.e., that all phenomena are manifestations of matter and that these manifestations can be tested and verified by predictable laws. Rational materialism might be a more accurate term for O'Donoghue's theorisation given that his argument seems to contest purely materialistic notions of reality.

1996, 154) to the supposed Irish intellectual "deficit" as signified by the tenacity of popular culture and Catholic religious belief. With "'civilization' [defined and circumscribed] within what comprises writing" (de Certeau 1988, 184), it follows that the rationality of print culture was seen as essential to the "civilizing" influence advanced by the colonialist project. The tenacious recalcitrance of orality thwarted the eradication of Irish "backwardness" however, as English writer William Makepeace Thackeray (1811-1863) outlined almost one hundred years after Hume's observations. In *The Irish Sketch Book* (1843), Thackeray laments the apparent inability of the burgeoning print culture in Ireland to completely eradicate the "'lies and tradition'" (Thackeray cited in Gibbons 1996, 146) perpetuated by "oral tradition and popular religious practice".

Rational materialism has formed the scientific and technological basis of the modern era, a rationality which limits the parameters of intellectually acceptable modern belief to the world that can be known literally and factually. Joyce's interpretations of life events as supernatural and Maher's fantastic fictions of the surreal broaden the contours of this reality so as to encompass the "inexplicable". Presenting worldviews that embrace the possibility of mystery and magic opens up the boundaries of a modern imagination that tends to valorize only what can be seen and verified, i.e., the visible over the hidden. In this sense, Joyce (2000) and Maher's (1998) elucidations of what O'Donoghue (1989, 2001) defines as "Celtic" belief not only underline the worldviews which both Ong (1967, 1991) and Eliade (1959, 1967) find common to oral cultures, but also reintroduce age-old beliefs that might be considered "archaic". However, these Traveller writers are simultaneously addressing contemporary environmental and social issues in ways that offer alternative paradigms for defining (and therefore inventing) Ireland in the modern world. In this way, their writing represents not an anachronism but an active challenge to accepted wisdom.

Oral influences are evident not only in Maher's inclusion of traditional Traveller ghost and wonder stories, but also in the facility with which Joyce incorporates incidents and occurrences – which she attributes to supernatural causes – into the "realism" of her "life story". On a first glance, Joyce's approach might be considered an odd strategy considering that she wishes to convince the reader of the reliability of her account. Although these transitions between the ordinary and the extraordinary are presented as a natural facet of her daily life, their unusual content disrupts the reader's expectations of a realist text. Maher's miracle stories and Joyce's mysticism integrate "rationality" and "irrationality" by dissolving the boundary between the natural and the supernatural in ways that flout the rationalist Enlightenment worldview (Cavallaro 2001, 44).[4]

What makes one set of "beliefs" acceptable while another set is judged superstitious? In the modern era, one factor seems to correlate with how far removed "practice" is from "daily life". De Certeau (1988) notes that while "'de-Christianization'" (1988, 183) occurred with the Enlightenment, this could be more accurately defined as "a deterioration of the religious universe [since] Christian faith is still compatible with this disappearance" (1988, 183). The nature of what was deemed "acceptable" religious practice and belief also changed.[5] This growing distance between the experiential and the theoretical was increasingly reflected in the absence "of references to real local life" (de Certeau 1988, 189). Religious belief as expressed through a close connection with daily life reflects the immediacy of orality and was increasingly deemed as "regressive", while beliefs based on an abstract or distant "law-giver" / "law-maker" as reflective of literate modes of knowing were deemed more enlightened. Irish history provides a fairly recent example of modernist / anti-modernist ruptures that resulted in the division of knowledge between "acceptable" and "unacceptable" forms. In Ireland, this break with the past paralleled the destruction of the hegemony of colonisation and was born out of the devastation of the Great Famine. The loss and dislocation generated as a consequence of this national catastrophe were, in part, expressed through an extensive rejection of traditional modes of thought and belief.

To be considered "respectable" and to gain social advancement within a colonized nation requires "appropriating the culture of the colonizer" (Bourke 1995, 4). Bourke (1995, 1996) observes that in the Ireland of the post-Famine era, an urban Catholic middle-class distanced itself from the "benightedness" of the past – that the catastrophic Famine seemed to epitomize – by rejecting traditional "folk" beliefs. She also suggests that language issues played a crucial role in this transformation as the Irish middle-class embraced "literacy, rather than orality; English rather than the Irish language" (1995, 4).

Popular modes of worship fell out of favour within the established churches as modernization in post-famine Ireland was paralleled in the

[4] So too do the maintenance of "traditional" Catholic practices, including the Traveller veneration of holy wells and other religious traditions sometimes regarded by non-Travellers as residues of superstition.

[5] Examining the "official clerical discourse" of Christianity in France after the Revolution, de Certeau (1988) finds that as priests became more learned, religious discourse became more "uniform and without internal contradictions; it was ruled by quotation, impermeable to personal experience" (de Certeau 1988, 189).

religious sphere by centralizing within the Roman Catholic Church, in particular. This impulsion sought to "exorcise the baneful influence of traditional cultural practices (such as wakes, "keening", "patterns" at holy wells, and other "pagan" rituals) from religious devotions, bringing Irish Catholicism into line with *Roman* Catholic orthodoxy" (Gibbons 1996, 136). In spite of the "suppression" of traditional devotions and rituals originating in pre-Christian customs Travellers are an Irish "other" who continue to practice certain outward demonstrations of faith as attendance at particular pilgrimages and holy wells.[6]

Landscapes Haunted by History

In Ireland, sacred places have become interconnected with its colonial history. Poets such as Eavan Boland (see portions of Boland's poem, "The Colonists" cited above) and Seamus Heaney[7] have utilized the figure of a landscape haunted by its history. Seán's mother's holy wells stories not only support this trope but also emphasize the notion of a landscape sanctified by (religio-political) martyrdom.

Maher weaves various incidents and events with stories of historical and cultural trauma – both personal and collective – explanations of human suffering that may go some way towards assuaging his own personal pain, and the history of his troubled and lonely childhood. At least one prayer he relates indicates that he suffered many disappointments as a child. The child Seán prays, "'God, why don't you make my father like me? Why don't you stop him from fighting with my mother over me? She always sticks up for me, but when she does my father beats her. This isn't fair, Lord. Why do you let it happen?'" (1998, 73). Maher concludes,

---

[6] These devotions involve an "annual pilgrimage … on the feast day of the patron saint of the parish" (Ní Dhomhnaill 1996, 423) to a location associated with the saint, a site established through tradition. Many of these sacred places have pre-Christian, even druidic origins, and are therefore strongly associated with nature, with an emphasis on the hallowedness of the location. Those places that are still visited are numerous. Some are based on ancient traditions, such as Tara, once considered the *omphalos* of the world, and are identifiable by archaeological evidence. Besides these locations, other sites such as tree groves formed natural structures used for worship. Knowledge of at least some of these natural sites remains in popular memory. The criteria by which druidic wisdom chose these sites seems to have had to do with telluric lines, the belief that these junctures coincided with portals into the other worlds presumed to parallel the physical / temporal world of human experience.

[7] See, for example, Seamus Heaney's "The Strand at Lough Beg", originally published in *Field Work* (1979).

wryly, "But even God, it seemed then, hadn't the answer to my questions" (1998, 73). This child's view[8] of God's direct intervention in human affairs is one which was (at least partly) instilled by his mother. While Maher distances himself from his characters' views, apocalyptic language recurs often enough in *The Road to God Knows Where* to reflect a distinct sense of despair on the part of the writer / narrator.

Gibbons argues that "'in conditions of acute stress' … [a] blurring of the boundaries between the personal and the political" occurs (Gibbons citing Miroslav Hroch 1996, 21) whereby the individual identifies so strongly with national trauma that this trauma becomes almost personalised. Accordingly, Maher's response to communal catastrophe integrates not only Ireland's ordeal under colonial oppression, or that of the Travellers as a persecuted people, but also his unresolved childhood trauma that can only be expressed in more depersonalized terms. Tales of martyrdom predominate in "marginal" communities "confronted with the threat of extinction", de Certeau (1988, 273) argues, and the proliferation of such stories among Maher's (1998) characters suggests a community that feels under siege.

Thematically, his story continues with the description of hardships and anecdotes that would be both inexplicable and unbearable were they not justified by a sense that sacrifice contributes to the greater good and the renewal of faith amongst believers. Such a belief is buoyed by a faith in the hereafter where martyrdom will be rewarded. His mother's stories recall a time of religious persecution when the Penal Laws made it illegal for Catholics to meet and when they "'could not say Mass in public … they had to find secret places to say it'" (1998, 85). The congregation (there were Travellers among them) is discovered as they worship by the well and, along with the priest, they "'were murdered in cold blood by a band of soldiers'" (1998, 85). Within the conventions of a martyrdom tale, the soldiers, as emissaries of the colonial power, represent the "devil" (de Certeau 1988, 273). Garrard (2004) notes that a tone of "extreme moral dualism" (2004, 86) typifies apocalyptic language. Accordingly, Maher's mother uses an emotionally-charged language that sets a clear-cut distinction between good and evil, i.e., that vilifies the "persecutors" and beatifies the martyred. The first section of her narrative concludes with an atrocity that underscores the barbarity of the colonial oppressors, "'The

---

[8] If Maher (the writer's) views have changed since childhood, he does not indicate this.

priest, God bless him, was tortured before his body was cut in pieces'" (1998, 85), at a place named Colaney Well.[9]

In her proleptic conclusion, his mother anticipates and dismisses any logical explanations for the existence of the well but focuses on the supernatural aspects of the story, "'Of course a lot of people will say that there is a spring going up the trunk of the tree … and that's why it stays full, but if this was the case the well would overflow; it never overflows nor goes dry'" (1998, 88). Her story concludes with the formulaic, "'there you are children … that's the true story of Colaney Well'" (1998, 88), a reminder that orality is the medium which underscores Traveller culture and intergenerational transmission within the community. While Maher (1998) may wish to create a record of his community's traditional belief, he views such beliefs as a partial "outsider" and with the scepticism afforded by his scholarly education. This "in-between" status exacerbates the sense of alienation and the feeling of profound loneliness that pervades his memoir.

The Bane of Modernity and Apocalyptic Consolations

Maher feels like an outsider amongst his fellow Travellers. Similarly, Travellers feel and are treated as "outsiders" within the nation. Thus, Maher lives in a double "solitude". He responds to this dilemma by presenting Traveller "perspectives" that expose social contradictions within modern capitalist democracies, inconsistencies within societies that profess equality as a value even while disadvantaged groups are systematically excluded. Maher does not promote any "obvious" political agenda, yet after he has left home, his characters try to "educate" him in "the ways of the world" and this leads to heated discussions and invectives against perceived injustices. His emphasis on storytelling gives the appearance of being apolitical while the fictional style gives his characters the freedom to declare their views with little or no editorial input, a strategy that permits the writer room for exploration without commitment.

[9] Maher's mother does not give the timeframe of this event though historically it would have been between 1691 and the Rebellion of 1798, the year of the next account when a second priest is martyred. The irony of the second martyrdom is that the faithful were commemorating the earlier massacre at the same well. Their death as they worshipped confirms the sanctity of their spilled blood. Having complied with the rhetorical necessity of grounding the introduction in historical events that authenticate the sacredness of the well through martyrdom, her story concludes with a "miracle" that employs religious iconography.

Maher remains the "master" storyteller – the sense of being the creator of the space in which these "actors" express themselves in – while his characters appear autonomous. In allowing expression to these diverse points of view, Maher gives voice to those people excluded from the benefits of economic progress and for whom "modernity" may represent a form of loss. These perspectives counterbalance dominant discourses and challenge conceptions which the "majority" community may take for granted. Through such a process, Maher is free to offer "radically new perspectives on basic historical categories and values, such as 'work,' 'progress,' and 'justice'" (Stone-Mediatore 2003, 122).

While Joyce (2000) is the more overtly "political" writer, Maher (1998) nevertheless articulates quite a radical language through the medium of his characters. Both the doll-man and his own mother use apocalyptic language to express and to explain their dire "social" situation. Their extreme pessimism confirms Thompson's (1997) appraisal of "[a]pocalypticism … as a genre born out of crisis" (Thompson cited in Garrard 2004, 86). Language is polarized and depicts a moral "struggle between good and evil" (Thompson cited in Garrard 2004, 86). While Garrard notes that Christian millenarianism "stresses radical discontinuity" (2004, 88), an ahistoricism that releases the believer from engagement in political or temporal governments, such views are by no means apolitical in nature. Even if proponents choose to opt out of the then present systems they find themselves functioning within, apocalypticism is still a political stance. Examining the doll-man's anti-modernist diatribe as a product of the social reality that generates it helps to shed further light on the exact nature of the grim prognostications that are put forward concerning the future destiny of the Traveller community.

Maher met the doll-man when he and his wife befriended the twelve-year-old Seán after he ran away from his parents. The couple were acquainted with Maher's parents and knew of his father's drinking. This character's nickname comes from the unique way in which the doll-man makes a living. The couple travelled from town to town and in each town the doll-man would give a performance using his hand-cart as a stage and featuring his hand-made, "dancing" marionette to the accompaniment of a mechanical music box that required winding. In a culture where elderly people are rare, the doll-man, "nearly seventy-six years of age" (1998, 103), is one of life's survivors. His experience and viewpoint are from an earlier generation; he speaks of times from before World War I, for example. In his lifetime, therefore, he has seen great changes, including the tumultuous transition from colonial rule to the founding of the Irish Republic after the Irish Civil War (1922). Maher (1998) distances himself from the doll-man's views by presenting them as the jeremiad of an old man and offers no opinion on them, though reasonably, being part of his memoir, they are formative to his identity in some way. Only in the closing pages when he writes of "the horribleness of modern ethics and thinking" (1998, 164), does Maher openly articulate his own views regarding modernity, although these could have been previously divined due to the propagation of similar "anti-modern" espousals from his characters. At this juncture, Maher admits that the "great influence" the doll-man had over him was as valuable as "whatever learning I got in the years afterwards" (1998, 100), an appraisal that encompasses his brief years of formal education. In the doll-man's version of literary history, Chaucer, Shakespeare and other "great figures of literature" (1998, 100) were either Travellers or gleaned their stories and derived their inspiration from Traveller tales. He goes further in attributing an ancient and honourable lineage, tracing Traveller origins to "the days of the kings of Ireland and their clans" (1998, 105).

These are the kinds of claims that Lanters seems to dismiss when she writes: "Travellers sometimes endow themselves with respectable ancestors by casting important cultural and historical figures into the role of Travellers" (2005, 28). While Lanters does acknowledge the symbolic value of such claims, her interpretation seems to exclude the possibility of any factual basis for such assertions, even though historically, more privileged artists, writers and musicians (i.e., those who enjoy the benefits of a broader cultural education that reflect a more mainstream status), appropriate "folk" tales, songs and imagery from minority cultures around the world. Regarding this issue, Canadian Roma writer, Ronald Lee, opens his "autobiographical novel", *Goddam Gypsy*, on the subject of appropriation framed as an accusation: "Our music, our art, our crafts, our fashions have been stolen to be presented in the concert halls and museums of the world … All that we have created through the centuries has been taken from us, and yet in popular myth we are the 'thieves'" (no pagination)[10]. Far from dismissing the doll-man, Seán believes in the rich cultural heritage of Travellers, even though this is not affirmed in any way by what he learns at school.

---

[10] First Nations writers in Canada have expressed similar grievances. See *The Globe and Mail*, Jan. 26, 1990, "Stop Stealing Native Stories," by Lenore Keeshig-Tobias (1990), as one example. Because the issue involves questions of ownership as based on power differentials, the practice is ongoing and unlikely to be discontinued anytime soon. In spite of this pessimistic assessment, the worldwide web remains a potential force for equality since it allows less advantaged groups a public forum.

The doll-man's tales of a vibrant Traveller culture from a glorious and mythical past creates an even sharper juxtaposition when compared to the poverty of their present-day living conditions. The doll-man exposes the inherent contradictions of a modernising society when he censures "'the so-called progress of the nation'" (Maher 1998, 105) for bringing harm to Travellers, "'I see the great injustice that is being done to all our people on the road … The only progress for those on the road is misery, suffering and abuse'" (1998, 105). This negative assessment of modernity points to the fact that economic or social progress does not necessarily imploy upon marginalized groups such as Travellers. Instead, long-marginalized groups often tend to "remain in poverty", and may even experience further difficulties or repression by being displaced or otherwise "debilitated by 'development'", and this with "little legal or political" recourse (Stone-Mediatore 2003, 180). By depicting progress as a loss, Traveller perspectives expose the human cost of so-called progress for more marginalized individuals or groups who may be negatively impacted through dislocation or loss of traditional livelihood, etc. Though Maher is less overtly political, the dollman's invective against the "evils" of modernity remains firmly grounded in a social context and reveals the trauma of everyday prejudice that may give rise to apocalyptic visions – which may seem a "solace" for the subjugated. Experiencing "progress" as a loss of tradition and economic independence, the doll-man laments the decline in civility concomitant with increased affluence when he observes, "'For all the education and all the so-called prosperity, simplicity, love and human understanding have walked out the door'" (1998, 105).

On three separate occasions the doll-man blames the present problems of Travellers on "'this modern age'" (1998, 105), for which "plastic" becomes a synecdoche[11]. He laments the fact that he cannot save his own children from alcoholism, and blames "'the evil that is in modern society for their ruination'" (1998, 108). Thus, he redirects individualistic arguments that attribute all social ills to personal responsibility by placing Traveller problems within a broader social context.

Attendant with his gloomy assessment of the fundamental immorality of modernism, the doll-man predicts the destruction of the travelling way of life – "'like everything that is good in life, it's marked for doom'" (1998, 109) – thereby, transferring personal loss and its concomitant sense

[11] The development of disposable containers to package various items and materials represented a real loss of income for Travellers and thus becomes a tangible symbol of economic decline, as seen in Joyce's two-stanza poem (2000, 99).

of helplessness to the larger stage. Allegory[12] (such as apocalypticism represents) is an essential means for colonized people to express otherwise illicit points of view. Gibbons notes, "allegory in a colonized culture is part of the symbolic ordering of life itself and hence, for all its visionary tropes, is in a position to unmask power relations" (21). Edward Hayes (1855), referring to traditional Irish ballads, suggests, "'[t]he very extravagance of allegory employed … is an unmistakable index to the intensity of the persecution which produced it in the first place'" (Hayes cited in Gibbons 1996, 143). Disenchanted, disenfranchised, demoralized and disqualified from mainstream society, the frustration and alienation of marginalized groups fuels this apocalyptic language.

This apocalyptic theme, the imminent "destruction" of the Traveller community, is also conveyed in Maher's mother's story of St. Kevin. Her story again attributes deep spiritual qualities to the Travelling people, demonstrating that, in Ireland, so long "defined" by religion, Catholicism predominantly, the linking of one's forebears with such "foundational" and mythologized figures as St. Kevin establishes legitimacy. At the same time, it is a strategy which counters negative moral assessments and anti-Traveller prejudice as "constructed" by the majority population. At a loss for how to proceed with Christianizing Ireland, St. Kevin receives guidance through a vision that directs him to ask Traveller families camping nearby to assist him. From then on, his mission becomes very successful since the Travellers prove so adept at memorizing the Gospels and transmitting this knowledge as they travel the countryside. In this story, St. Kevin gathered the Travellers together just before he died and delivered a final sermon. The sermon begins by echoing Christ's sermon on the Second Coming in which Jesus foretells the destruction of Jerusalem and describes the last days: "For nation shall rise against nation, and kingdom against kingdom" (Mt. 24: 7)[13]. Similarly, St. Kevin predicts a gloomy future for humanity as a whole: "'[I]n my vision, I saw many dark and unholy deeds … king fighting king, nation fighting nation'"

[12] The use of allegory in Irish literature as a code to represent Irish resistance to English colonial oppression has a long history but as Lockett (2005) points out, the Irish Literary Revival also shaped this amorphous tradition into forms that served to mobilize nationalist sentiments. Yeats's play, *Cathleen ní Houlihan* (1902), "a conflation of mythology, folklore, and popular legend" (Lockett 2005, 5), depicts Ireland as an old hag who becomes a young beauty again when young Irish men sacrifice their lives to oust "the strangers in the house", the British, and regain "the four beautiful green fields", the four counties of Ireland (Yeats cited in Lockett 2005, 5).

[13] All Biblical quotes are from the King James Version of the Bible.

(1998, 83). His sermon establishes the Travellers as a special, holy or chosen people, but this honour necessitates that the Travellers will be subjected to the worst forms of ill treatment: "'In the vision I see them becoming a race of people apart, no longer the heralds of God, but instead humiliated and outcast beings'" (1998, 84). This pronouncement mirrors Lady Gregory's folk tale as outlined earlier since it legitimizes Traveller persecution as predestined, or sanctioned by God. In Maher's mother's tale this persecution is due not to any essentially "bad" character, but to the Travellers' adherence to the "one true faith".

Intertwining patriotism and religion, Maher's mother's apocalyptic stories imply that Traveller piety, far from being backwards, is a beacon for other Irish Catholics. Unlike the rest of Catholic Ireland who have embraced modernity, Travellers, in clinging to their traditions, are in fact cleaving to a truer faith. In order to understand the logic of this argument, one must remember that the English once perceived Ireland's Catholicism as a potential threat against the crown, a threat realized in the deposed Catholic monarch King James II's bid to regain the British throne by forming an allegiance with the French. This alliance ended on Irish soil with James's defeat by the Protestant king, William of Orange (William III) at the Battle of Boyne in 1690. If Catholicism was once perceived as an anti-English position, then Traveller contentions that they cleave to a truer, older Christianity aligns them with a long history of struggle and resistance against the historical colonial oppressor, an important distinction, especially given that the more modern, centralized Catholicism that Vatican Council 1870 inaugurated in Ireland promoted a turn away from nationalism as "popular insurgency" in favour of an "accommodation with state power" (Gibbons 1996, 136), which meant working with the colonial administration. Maher's storytellers' uncompromising rhetoric rejects any accommodation with the former colonial power, and Traveller resistance to modernity marks them out as "true patriots".

Maher's memoir (1998) is populated with people who espouse intensely political rhetoric, but not of the type that compels someone such as Joyce (2000) to become directly engaged in a political process. The mixture of religion and politics expressed by Maher's cohorts seems to give preference to spiritual solutions by assigning a possible spiritual significance and resolution to such practical problems as poverty. Though it does little to address poverty as a social condition with specific root causes and therefore, potential solutions, Maher's mother's story of St. Kevin explains the Travellers' poverty and outsider status in ways that have a positive angle, i.e., as a temporary trial that may have unspecified heavenly rewards although this latter point is not made explicit. This explanation recalls Christ's admonition, "Lay not up for yourselves treasures upon earth … But lay up for yourselves treasures in heaven" (Mat. 6: 19-20). One can see the influence here in Maher's writing of a "traditional" view for explaining poverty in the Catholic Ireland of his day. In Catholicism generally, poverty was often spiritualized in philosophical terms in the decades previous to this. Presented with Christ's lack of worldly success as a model to emulate, monastic initiates took vows of poverty, for example. Among the laity, "God's people" [14] were frequently depicted as those people who were blessed with poverty here on earth, as they would be rewarded in heaven. In Maher's text, the blessing of poverty is bestowed on the Travellers because they are spiritually strong enough to bear its physical sufferings and deprivations. St. Kevin foresees that "'even through this great degradation, humiliation, hate and persecution, the travelling people keep their great faith'" (1998, 83). Perhaps, because poverty had for so long been endemic among the Irish Catholics, an emphasis was placed on charitable works as an immediate, if temporary solution to paucity. Attributing a divine origin to present difficulties quells any idea of direct political involvement or action however, since, by this rationale, its potential solutions must be otherworldly in nature also. This turning away from practical solutions is also indicative of an utter disenchantment with "the-powers-that-be".

Thompson calls apocalypse, "the consolation of the persecuted", and notes that the intent of apocalyptic storytelling is to "stiffen the resolve of an embattled community by dangling in front of it the vision of a sudden and permanent release from its captivity" (Thompson cited in Garrard 2004, 86). Maher's mother's story serves this purpose to the extent that it ascribes a spiritual significance to hardships which encourages forbearance, but concludes by foretelling their utter obliteration as a people – surely a very pessimistic conclusion. Nevertheless, in this parable, there remains a divine purpose even to this horror because it is as

[14] The significance of this term, paraphrased in Joyce as "God's Children" was informed by an *Irish Nationalisms* class lecture given by Dana Hearne, Concordia University, Mar. 22, 2006. Note that the predominance of this paradigm is confined to a bygone era. Official Catholic attitudes towards poverty have always been diverse as evidenced in the philosophical writings of the Catholic Church throughout the centuries. In a joint study based on a survey analysis, Hardiman et al. (2006) introduce their findings with the precaution that while a "traditional view grounded in notions of charity is still widely expressed in social practice … some Catholic organisations advance distinctly radical and structural analyses of poverty. We are therefore unlikely to deduce any single *a priori* link between Catholicism and attitudes to poverty and wealth" (Hardiman et al. 2006, 4).

a result of this catastrophe that "'the hard-hearted people of Ireland'", along with the entire world, "'shall mourn the passing of the most unique race of people in the world'" (Maher 1998, 84). Just as the death of Christ was necessary in order to save the world, this story implies that a new and better world will emerge from the ashes of devastation, a devastation which culminates in a world without Travellers. Salvation through annihilation offers a grim inversion of the far-off hopes which a persecuted people lives through the prism of its own liberation narratives. Since Travellers are God's "chosen people", an element of hope remains, albeit for the "settled" community only, in the pledge that the destruction of the Travellers will bring about a spiritual revival – for "'the world will be renewed in faith and love of Almighty God'" (Maher 1998, 84). The apocalyptic scenarios propounded by Maher's characters leave Travellers little in the way of a definite "space" within the national narrative. Maher's stories define the Traveller role in Ireland as sacrificial and spiritually redemptive for the majority population, but leave Travellers (or at least their way of life) as doomed for extinction.

Traveller stories do not present the rational and the irrational as mutually exclusive polarities. Instead, the juxtaposition of both realism and the inexplicable in their narratives corresponds with similar conjunctions of the rational and irrational in every day life, even if such syntheses may appear contradictory at first glance. Eliade contends that modern secular individuals avoid facing the logical incongruities necessitated in conceiving themselves as "self-made" through "a series of denials and refusals" (Eliade 1959, 203-204). One typically evasive strategy is to categorize certain behaviours and beliefs as a form of "superstition" since the label is generally applied to the beliefs of others, and not to one's own. In addition to these cultural biases, Eliade identifies an essential contradiction within the "modern non-religious" individual. While the emphasis of secular democratic societies[15] is on individual "sovereignty", people nevertheless continue to practice desacralized myths and rituals (Eliade 1959, 203-4), often without acknowledging them or without even being aware of their sacred origins. Some of these behaviours reflect pre-Christian customs which invoked the magic of potent talismans for protection from harm. Christmas traditions such as

[15] While Eliade's observation can be said to be generally true in modern Western democracies, his assessment does not take into account the fundamental difference between highly secularized western European societies and American society, a nation whose puritanical origins often still dictate publicly espoused codes of political and social behaviour.

kissing under the mistletoe and bringing holly into the house may have druidic origins, for example.

This coalescence of the rational and irrational need not be regarded as an inherently negative development. Such syntheses can allow for a creative dynamic between the commonplace and the inexplicable, one which integrates diverse worldviews that are generally considered antithetical to one another. David Suzuki and co-author Peter Knudtson in their book *Wisdom of the Elders* (1992), here drawing on Claude Lévi-Strauss's proposal that a synthesis between the reductive approach of scientific enquiry which tends to fragment the world, and the holistic, or "totalizing" view of the "Native Mind"[16] (Suzuki and Knudtson 1992, 13) allows for more creative resolutions to difficulties caused by an over-reliance on modern technology. Orr (2002) attributes the narrow focus that is characteristic of both technological and scientific paradigms to "Descartes and Galileo" (Orr 2002, 20). He argues that "the foundations of the modern worldview were flawed from the beginning. In time, those seemingly small and trivial errors of perception, logic, and heart cascaded into a rising tide of cultural incoherence … and ecological degradation" (Orr 2002, 20). Suzuki (1997), citing Berry, expresses the need "to find a new story, a narrative that includes us in the continuum of Earth's time and space", a story that will "[remind] us of the destiny we share with all the planet's life" (Suzuki 1997, 25). Travellers, of course, are not "native in the sense that Strauss has delineated, i.e., non-white aboriginal cultures as yet relatively untouched by European influence. Nevertheless, in the era when Joyce and Maher were writing (i.e., within living memory), Travellers still maintained the close relationship with the land and its seasonal variations which Eliade highlighted as predominant in other contemporaneous rural European populations. Traveller writing reveals attitudes and aptitudes[17] which draw on this familiarity with the natural environment.

A worldview such as Joyce's understands the human and the natural worlds' spheres of activity as interrelated. Her contribution to ecological perspectives as outlined in her writing will be examined below as an offshoot of that worldview which rejects both hierarchies and hierarchical paradigms of leadership. Horizontal views of leadership offer more inclusive alternatives to the governance of hegemonic groups and therefore lie at the heart of democratic change. Another important feature

---

[16] Lévi-Strauss (1962) uses the term "savage mind".

[17] For example, many of the autobiographies in *Traveller Ways, Traveller Words* (1992) (works shaped by an interview process) reveal knowledge of "folk" remedies that utilize locally growing wild herbs.

of Joyce's worldview, and one which informs her experience of nature, lies in the belief that "the supernatural is indissolubly connected with the natural" (Eliade 1959, 118).

Modernity and Mystical Experience

Joyce's (2000) path to leadership begins with a tragedy, although she attributes her new-found confidence to a spiritual awakening that follows in its aftermath. While never explicitly articulated, the death of her first grandchild from meningitis seems to be the catalyst for Joyce to enter the realm of community activism. She speculates that the toddler contracted the disease that killed her from the rats which infested her family's camp during a rubbish strike when people dumped various items of rubbish, including medical waste on their site. This incident represents a "snapping" point that drives her to seek justice for her community. From this point on, her activism becomes more confident and more sophisticated in its approach. Joyce attributes her new-found strength to her strong religious faith.

Joyce offers various religious experiences that can only be described as "mystical" to explain her enhanced understanding of community, an understanding which grows to encompass a more inclusive and expansive sense of humanity in general. Immanence, i.e., her personal experience of God as a near and accessible presence, carries Joyce beyond the personal to a perspective which is more transpersonal. The force of Joyce's argument for Traveller equality (as full citizens) relies, in part, on establishing a sense of personal credibility. Joyce's use of anecdotes in which she attributes supernatural causes to events may seem an odd tactic in achieving this sense of credibility since such accounts disrupt the conventions of narrative "realism" that generally characterizes her text. Her revelations outline a worldview which allows for the possibility of supernatural causes to events which occur in the reality of the material world. This worldview is so meshed with day-to-day living that on those occasions when Joyce attributes supernatural significance to a particular event, it evolves so naturally as to almost seem a commonplace.

Joyce takes great care to ground these events within a physical reality in order to illustrate the manner whereby these occurrences take place in our everyday spatial / temporal plane. Such occurrences are therefore depicted as extraordinary without being beyond nature. This recalls the Celtic belief system whereby there exists more than one physical reality – i.e., that there are, in fact, various parallel realities that at times coincide with this – our earthly dimension. In recounting an otherworldly visitation on the night of her father's death, Joyce seems to affirm – without any sense of the dogmatic – a worldview whereby alternative dimensions may coincide with what we call reality. This idea challenges the reader in ways that may initially feel somewhat unsettling. One way in which some readers deal with this sense of discomfort is to ridicule or dismiss. Even if the reader ignores such stories or rationalizes them as fiction or the product of an over-active imagination, Joyce's propositions nevertheless counter the rational materialism that frequently pervades the modern worldview.

Joyce describes how when their mother was in hospital and their father had yet to return from visiting her, the children had to light the gas lamp themselves, a tricky task given that it had a tendency to flare up. With eight frightened children alone in a trailer on the unlit outskirts of a town, the three older children heard "a man scream, like someone dying" (2000, 41). They were camped beside a quarry and thought their father had fallen in, but they were too "afeard of the dark" to verify whether this was so. Next, Joyce says:

> A very strange thing happened. After we heard the scream someone came in the door. When you walk in a wagon the springs go down and the wagon shakes; we could feel the pressure on the door and the floor moving but we couldn't see anyone. We heard footsteps, the wagon went down a little bit — and the Tilley lamp was turned off. (2000, 41-2)

Though her account is grounded in the physical world, she interprets these phenomena in a paranormal fashion. In addition to detailing the physical characteristics of a caravan, thereby establishing the setting as a material reality, Joyce employs the three primary sensory perceptions to establish veracity: the kinesthetic (i.e., an awareness of one's body in space); hearing – the scream and the footsteps; and sight – a sense accentuated by its ineffectuality in this darkened environment. With the light extinguished, they are left in the total darkness of the void. Though they cannot *see* with their eyes, they can nevertheless "sense" a presence. This anecdote provides a medium for expressing the inexpressible. When she concludes this account with, "I was always thinking about the scream we heard at the same time Father was in the [police] cell" (2000, 42), she circumscribes this event without delineating the catastrophic, emotional impact of her father's unsolved death, where a more expository approach might only confirm the ineffability of certain aspects of human experience. The sudden appearance of the inexplicable not only unsettles the usual expectations of a realist text, but also serves to reject the imperatives of a Western materialism that would discount the inference (never actually articulated) that their father's ghost visited them the night of his death.[18] Although this would be extraordinary, this visitation is by no means represented as a rift in the natural order of things. Joyce does not try to convince the reader to believe that spirits of the deceased can return. She merely relates these events as she experienced them, and leaves the reader to interpret them as he / she so wishes. However, every experience that Joyce imbues with a significance beyond the commonplace has a deep and often lasting impact upon her. This is especially true of the experience that occurs in the wake of the stress and emotion which follow her granddaughter's death.

In examining the implications of Joyce's spiritual experiences, it is important to note the difficult material circumstances which seem to initiate these moments of religious revelation, i.e., periods of vulnerability, extreme stress and depression, all factors leading to or symptoms of what has come to be known as "mental illness". In one such instance, Joyce is alone, having just collected her second baby from a convalescent hospital where the baby was recovering from a hernia operation. Still holding the infant in her arms, Joyce experiences an episode of amnesia. "[M]y mind just went", she writes, "My memory was gone. It must have been the effects of the birth because I wasn't really well for a long time after … I didn't know what I was standing there for or where the child came from" (2000, 68). She seeks help from a clerk in a nearby pharmacy only to be ignored. Joyce identifies the aversion which the average person experiences when confronted with a stranger in distress by concluding, "I suppose she thought I was mental" (2000, 68). Next she goes into a nearby chapel where her memory returns when she "[lights] some candles and [starts] to pray" (2000, 68). "I thanked God when everything came back into my mind — at least I knew the way home" (2000, 68), she adds.

Her granddaughter's death was another event which led to a great deal of emotional turmoil in the extended family. Joyce coped with this by taking action. Seeing her daughter's anguish, and feeling that "'too many people got away with too many things in my lifetime'" (2000, 90), Joyce began to build a case against the attending physician who had failed to properly diagnose and treat the child when her parents brought her to the hospital. By the time they returned again that evening, it was too late to

[18] O'Donoghue (1989, 2001) identifies characteristic ancient Irish beliefs that were popularly known through a strong oral tradition of stories and legends. One is a belief that there are other realities besides the world with which we are familiar, parallel worlds with permeable boundaries. This allows for the possibility that the deceased are "in some sense still present with family and friends" (O'Donoghue 2001, 37).

save her life. When Joyce returned to the hospital to find out the name of the doctor, the sister[19] who was in charge would not provide his name. Joyce was outraged by this and rejected the woman's fatalistic attitude: "[W]hat did she say to me? 'It's all the will of God'!" (2000, 90).

When Mary (the bereaved mother) had a nervous breakdown and was admitted "to the nerve hospital" (2000, 90), Joyce no longer had the time nor energy to keep fighting to prove medical negligence as contributing to her granddaughter's death and therefore, she dropped the legal case. Visiting her daughter at the asylum and seeing the other mental patients, many of them young women, Joyce has an "epiphany" that leaves her with a sense of deep compassion for others and an acceptance of human frailty as part of life, "Life can turn you if you haven't got strong will-power." An outpouring of sympathy and empathy with the suffering overcomes her: "I know it's not right to feel sorry for people because I hate pity myself, but I started crying because it broke my heart looking at them" (2000, 91). This "epiphany" occurs in the interstices of her composing a poem. Observing the women around her, and with the sunlight momentarily blinding her eyes, she says:

> I always carry a little diary in my pocket … I had just started writing a little poem about looking at those women when strong sun came in my eyes and I couldn't see a ha'porth. Someone who didn't believe in God would never believe me but I got a funny feeling that God was very close, that he was closer to the asylum than he was to any other place. (2000, 91)

The last line echoes a Christian (Catholic) belief that God bestows a special dispensation on the lowly and downtrodden, and also demonstrates her identification and empathy with these women. A true compassion requires being able to see oneself in the other. Although her idiom here is her own distinct "conversational" style, her feeling of inclusiveness and wholeness here is similar to that experienced by religious devotees and initiates around the world. Like them, her experience or "epiphany" in this moment of crisis generates a sense of inclusiveness which permits her to transcend more limited and negative points of view and the circumstances she then finds herself in (Greyson and Liester 2004, 321). From this point onwards, Joyce's narrative increasingly describes herself in terms of someone who is able to help other people, a principle of leadership as service, one articulated here when she looks around at these young women "all gathered round me" (2000, 91). Her comment, "I'm that kind of

---

[19] At this time, many of Ireland's institutions, including hospitals, were still administrated by Catholic religious communities.

person" (2000, 91), expresses an enhanced awareness of this aspect of her character not previously articulated in the text. She expresses a new awareness of differences between individuals without employing the hierarchical distinctions and judgements of difference which place more value on some individuals over others. While she is conscious of her own strength of character, she nevertheless understands that this does not give her licence to find fault with others – but to be more tolerant instead: "I've always had this will-power that I can get up and fight on again, but we're not all as strong as each other and people who give up can't help it" (2000, 91). Her personal hardships have (most likely) moulded her in a certain manner and informed these new insights. This worldview offers an alternative to those more conventional forms of leadership that are based on the individualist model. Hierarchical models stress privilege and status whereas Joyce's conception of her leadership-as-service places more emphasis on "horizontal" relationships as based on principles of equality.

The psychiatric hospital provides a setting which resonates with the historical reverberations of "madness" and "otherness" as expressed in popular literature but one which does not attempt to address previous connections between the two modes, nor how the Western tradition has come to define "mental illness". It should be noted that Joyce's practice of writing in her journal at this instant bypasses earlier models of psychoanalysis[20] which worked with the assumption that the patient required a professional "guide" – i.e., the psychoanalyst – in order to understand the hidden workings of the subconscious. Writing one's life history represents a departure from this previous hierarchical patient / professional relationship as Joyce's journal symbolizes. Today, building on the ideas of cognitive therapy[21], psychologists focus increasingly on the "stories" we tell ourselves, believing that these self-narratives can be rewritten in ways that are both positive and helpful. By emphasizing self-writing as self-knowledge, autobiographical theorist Paul John Eakin

---

[20] Foucault's work in deconstructing the patient / doctor relation as a relationship of power (see for example *Abnormal: Lectures at the Collège de France 1974-1975* (2003) as a partial summary of his life's work to that date) helped to spur an "anti-psychiatry" movement which attempted to equalize the relationship and of which Jerome Bruner's approach can be considered a part.

[21] "The goal of cognitive therapy is to identify maladaptive ways of thinking and replace them with adaptive ways that provide a more effective base for coping with the real world" (Gray 1994, 665).

(1999) has applied Jerome Bruner's "'narrative'" (1999, 21) psychology[22] in his study of autobiography and identity, *How Our Lives Become Stories: Making Selves*. Rakow and Wackwitz (2004) have arrived at similar conclusions: – "we must remember ourselves and represent our identity and past experiences to ourselves with interpretive frameworks that connect and make sense of our own biographies (i.e., stories we tell ourselves about ourselves)" (2004, 173). Rakow and Wackwitz (2004) explain the process whereby a self-identity is constructed, while cognitive therapy recognizes the debilitating, limiting, and sometimes falsity of our self-narratives in addition to their potential for the reinterpretation and re-writing of our lives. Thus, while all narratives involve a process of selection that depends on a particular framework of interpretation, any or all of these elements may change.

That Joyce's "religious experience" occurs while visiting a hospital for psychiatric patients recalls the whole history of evolving attitudes towards "mental illness" which Foucault explored at length in *Madness and Civilization (1965).* In *Madness and Civilization (1965)*, analysing Cervantes' *Don Quixote* and Shakespeare's *King Lear*, Foucault brought to light a pre-Enlightenment view where what was defined as "madness" still retained "a link with the sacred" (Hayes 1996, 2). Foucault introduces *Madness and Civilization* with an analysis of the profusion of early modern literary and visual images which, he argues, indicated the "proliferation of meaning" (Foucault 1965, 18) attributed to "madness" in the 15th and 16th centuries. Foucault outlined how, from the Enlightenment onwards, aberrant behaviours formerly ascribed to demonic (or divine) influences, were now delineated within the emerging science of "mental" illness which "demystified" the human mind. This altered perception precluded the possibility that the "mad" were (potentially) in possession of a divine knowledge unavailable to ordinary people – i.e., "the literary madman [as] … a disguised philosopher" (Felman 1975, 207) that early modern writers had sometimes allowed for. While Joyce does not explore these historical reverberations, there is no doubt that the circumstances of her religious awakening resonate with some of these significations and motifs.

---

[22] "Jerome Bruner and other narrative psychologists" [believe] that self-narration is the defining act of the human subject, an act which is … "fundamental to the emergence and reality of that subject" (Eakin citing Kerby 1999, 21).

Studying the lives of the saints, one might conclude that the difference between religious experience and psychosis[23] can, on occasion, be difficult to delineate. One of the defining characteristics of the religious experience is that it is attributed by the recipient to powers outside of themselves, and tends to have a lasting and positive impact. Though scientific studies of these phenomena are limited, as of yet, a survey of participants who experienced "nonpathological auditory hallucinations" (Greyson and Liester 2004, 322) discovered that the "majority" (2004, 328-9) of respondents felt positively about their experience. The study summarises its conclusions as follows: "Nonpathological auditory hallucinations differ from psychotic hallucinations in that they tend to be supportive rather than critical; they may offer truths with a validity beyond the limits of the ego; they generally enhance personal, interpersonal, and societal functioning" (Greyson and Liester 2004, 322). While Joyce does not claim to "hear voices" during her "epiphany", she has in common with the phenomena studied by Greyson and Liester (2004) that her experience leads to a permanent and positive change typical of these kinds of experiences (Greyson and Liester 2004, 323).

Joyce is momentarily blinded by an intense light during her "epiphanic" moment, reminiscent of a metaphor that recurs in other famous "conversion" stories – the biblical account of Paul on the road to Damascus, for instance. Is physical blindness meant to dramatize a lack of spiritual discernment or do such stories suggest the opposite, i.e., is temporary physical blindness a necessary precondition to true spiritual insight?

Ong (1967, 1991) has argued that the reliance on visual literacy in the form of writing required the objectification of language. The door to scientific objectivity was opened through literacy, issuing in a fundamental change in the way people see themselves in relation to the world. Sight is a "dissecting sense" since it "situates the observer outside what he views" (Ong 1991, 72). In contrast with this, experiencing language as sound makes the listener the "centre of [his or her] auditory world" (Ong 1991, 72) with the result that oral cultures retain a sense of the world wherein they are still active participants. Eliade (1959, 1967) has a slightly different view of the oral / literacy dichotomy and attributes a worldview such as Joyce's to the "archaic" belief that "*the world exists because it was created by the gods*" (Eliade's italics 1959, 165). While Eliade uses the plural here, "gods" can equally invoke the monotheistic

[23] Jovanovic (1993) cites Michel's (1986) study of Catherine de Pazzi that proposed a diagnosis of sadomasochism (Jovanovic 1993, 242-3). He also cites other authors who contend such diagnoses.

God as creator conceived in "Celtic Christianity" – a form of spirituality that is so eloquently expressed in earliest Irish language poetry. This supernatural dimension is rooted in the belief of the world as God's creation (Eliade 1959, 165). When people view "the whole of life [as] capable of being sanctified", life takes on an extra dimension of meanings (Eliade 1959, 167). As Eliade explains, "life is lived on a twofold plane; it takes its course as human existence and, at the same time, shares in a transhuman life, that of the cosmos or the gods" (1959, 167). The world becomes a "text" in which God, the gods or the Spirit is revealed. Suzuki and Knudtson (1992) outline a similar worldview, one where all natural things are alive and worthy of respect because we as humans share a "kinship" with our fellow creatures. There is a sense of participating in a world that is teeming with different forms of life – including humanity – as well as "insentient" life forms e.g., trees[24], (Suzuki & Knudtson 1992, xxxii), and also what we view as "non-living things": rocks, rivers and the earth itself (see Suzuki and Knudtson 1992, 34). "Traditional" cultures which ascribe to such a worldview frequently relate to other life forms with "a profound sense of empathy and kinship … rather than [with] a sense of separateness from them or superiority over them" (Suzuki and Knudtson 1992, 18). Such a relationship as based on a new sense of equality and kinship are mirrored in Joyce's sense of oneness as represented in such moving scenes as her visit to the sick women in hospital.

Another encounter which moves Joyce deeply also suggests her awareness of the non-human world and its intricate relation with that which is human. As with other similar stories, Joyce hints that she was then at a low point in her life and that it was a struggle just to get out of bed. Her focus is on the physical symptoms of her condition at this point rather than her emotions: "I was very sick and all my strength had gone. I was so run-down and tired I had the feeling I was finished" (2000, 95). She walks into a nearby field to pray and be alone, "crying at the one time" (2000, 95) and it is here that she experiences a number of physical sensations that may include symptoms of a fever. Once again, the association between a weakened physical condition and revelation corresponds with much traditional "mystic" discourse[25]. "All of a sudden I got this burning on top of my head. I thought it was on fire. I put up my

[24] Or "tree people" as the Haida, a First Nations people of the Canadian Pacific coast, call trees.

[25] Julian of Norwich (1342-1416) was "mortally ill" (Gilmore 1994, 114) at the time of her visions. Often, as with Catherine of Sienna (Jovanovic 1993), sickness is self-imposed through excessive fasting and other extreme ascetic practices.

hand beside my forehead and I could feel the heat going through my fingers" (2000, 95). This description echoes a beautifully expressed line of a medieval Irish poem: "I am the God who created the fire in the head" (Finan 1989, 78). Such images recall the day of Pentecost where the giving of the Holy Spirit is described as "cloven tongues like as of fire, and it sat upon each of [the faithful assembled]" (Acts 2: 3). Reading Joyce's text in this moment, the bird that Joyce describes as follows: "It wasn't really a natural bird like a pigeon or a crow or a pheasant, it was a big bluey-grey bird. When it was flapping its wings where I was sitting its feathers were falling down and some of them fell in my lap" (2000, 96), would be analogous with the Holy Spirit, usually represented by a dove, making this, in a certain sense, a blending of "pagan" and Christian motifs. Although Joyce offers a natural explanation for the sudden appearance of this bird, "it must have been nesting and maybe I disturbed it," she simultaneously attributes an origin outside of nature. The bird startles her with its "awful noise, flapping its wings," so that she feels afraid: "I got a terrible shock altogether and I didn't know whether to run out of the field or what" (2000, 96). This combination of fear and amazement evokes "the sublime", an expression that is almost "spiritual" in nature. The evocation of mood here bears many similarities with the discourse of European Romanticism, which itself, was a response to the "rationalistic order" of modernity (Salerno 2003, 195). These Romantics employed the sublime in nature in order to re-create a mystical experience to an increasingly secular population. To merely acknowledge European precedents would obviate the insights that the Romantic Movement imbibed from their knowledge of indigenous European and non-European cultures[26] around them.

Although Joyce's fearful reaction suggests that she does not fully understand the exact nature of this incident (she "hurried" out of the field

---

[26] European Romantic writers and composers plundered the stories and songs of European "folk" cultures. As noted by Romany writer Ronald Lee in his autobiographical novel, *Goddam Gypsy* (1971), this included "Gypsy" stories, songs (see Johannes Brahms and Franz Liszt's Hungarian Dances), and visual imagery. Such borrowing was inspired by Rousseau's "noble savage", the notion of prelapsarian Man, in itself a romanticized viewpoint. However, in spite of this romanticism, there is no doubt that after almost two hundred years of cross-cultural contact with the indigenous peoples of colonized lands, Europeans had some understanding of aboriginal ways. This debt has only recently begun to be investigated by academics but much work remains to be done. Bruce E. Johansen's PhD. Dissertation (published as *Forgotten Founders* (1987)) explores the influence that the political and social structure of the League of the Ho-de-no-sau-nee or Iroquois Nations had on the American Founding Fathers as they formulated the American Constitution.

and felt "shaky over the experience"(2000, 96)) – she nevertheless attaches a strong significance to this encounter with the natural world, a significance which one associates with other orally based traditions.[27]

The emphasis among oral cultures on life "as lived", as opposed to the reliance on abstract theory, necessitates that spiritual matters always retain an intrinsically practical aspect. In *My Life on the Road* (2000), this is evidenced by Joyce's response to her strange encounter with the bird. She immediately applies herself to the household tasks she had neglected because of her depressed state with renewed vigour. Although she engages in ordinary, everyday tasks, Joyce now describes a feeling that approximates to a form of elation: "I got this strength that I could go through anything and nothing could stop me" (2000, 96). Interestingly, she does not describe this experience encompassing a sudden change of mood and emotion as anything unusual: "I've had loads of experiences like this in my life — I suppose it happens to loads of people" (2000, 96). Her experience has effected a profound transformation, however, as Joyce indicates – "I felt a different person: I felt brand-new" (2000, 96). Joyce immediately immerses herself in the daily routine of activities, thereby maintaining the connection with "the events of everyday life" (2000, 8) that Ó Duinn (2000) finds typifies "Celtic Christianity".

In summary, Joyce's mystical experiences and the meanings she associates with them suggest the strong possibility that there are different types of human experience, many of which defy purely physiological, materialist categories. As the Greyson study (2004) has suggested, faith in a higher power[28] can help alleviate depression and certain other common

---

[27] This exchange between the human and the natural worlds bears strong allusions to the magical world of fairy tales, originally an oral genre, in addition to First Nations stories of encounters between animals and practitioners of traditional "medicine" healers whose special gifts often included an ability to communicate with other species. There are often quite literal analogies between the human and the nonhuman entities in these stories. (See Blondin, *When the World Was New: Stories of the Sahtú Dene* (Yellowknife: Outcrop, The Northern Publishers, 1990), for example.) First Nations stories often concern immediate survival issues and involve codes of right behaviour. Favours or powers are conferred by the totem animal on the human, often symbolized by the proffering of a talisman (such as feathers) along with supernatural abilities that designate the human as shamans (healers) among their people. Recognizing relationships between different species as not only possible but beneficial conforms with Eliade's observation that in such worldviews, "life … is not strictly confined to man's mode of being" (1959, 166); importance is also accorded to non-humans.

[28] Faith in something beyond oneself in part implies an ability to be able to attribute a meaning to life's vicissitudes beyond one's personal perspective.

(present-day) psychological symptoms, including anxiety. While Joyce represents her Catholic faith as a fundamental aspect of her identity, she never fully rationalizes her "unusual" encounter with the bird, most probably because she is unable to do so. Neither does she identify this experience as a transformative one beyond a momentary euphoria and renewed vigour. She does conclude this segment of the book by recommending a spirit of thankfulness, however: "you need to thank [God] for the things you have", adding, even "if you have problems yourself you still don't know how lucky you are — you can always be worse off" (2000, 96). Learning to "count her blessings" undoubtedly derives from her trying life, but gratitude is also one of the basic attitudes of the Christian worldview.

While many present-day readers of Joyce's text might be tempted to view the "religious" / "spiritual" experience with the bird as a lapse in rationality, it may be more instructive to reflect on the manner whereby rationality and the inexplicable coexist. Understanding this synthesis permits readings and points of view which move beyond a distinctly materialist rationale. Instead of dismissing this more intimate relationship with the natural world as quaint and archaic, a reading of Joyce's text that takes into account worldviews which inextricably link human activity as interconnected to the environment, permits an enhanced appreciation of these perspectives. Ong (1967, 1991) attributes this inter-connection between the human and natural worlds to the dialogistic dynamic that is at the heart of orality. He notes that dialogue "belongs to a culture which typically experiences problems as interconnected or simultaneous" (Ong 1967, 293), rather than "linear or sequential", a holistic approach to problem solving that engages "the entire human life-world" (Ong 1967, 294). A number of residual secondary oral cultures continue to survive in the present-day, e.g. the many different aboriginal and "indigenous" cultures; and the long tradition of orality as the legitimate medium for the transmission of knowledge reverberates still in both the Irish Traveller and non-Traveller cultures – as relating to storytelling, performance and song. The bardic tradition for which Ireland was once famous represented "vast amounts of [memorized] poetry, stories and historical material" (Flannery 1997, 18). The oral dissemination of this intricate, "tribal memory" has remained a strong cultural influence well into the modern era.

The Exultation of Nature: Fashioning a Place in the Irish Landscape

Although it is not included in her autobiography, Joyce's poem, "The Beauty I Can See", which appears in *Blackstones Around the Green Shamrock: A Poetry Anthology* (1994), is a modern variation on the "traditional" Irish nature poem, an important genre in Irish literature since the time when the *filidh* [29] first travelled the countryside. Related to the nature poem, but with a broader emphasis, Irish language poet, Nuala Ní Dhomhnaill (1996) has explored the tradition of *dinnsheanchas* (place-name lore) in Irish culture.[30] *Seanchas* encompasses all manner of lore, not only fairy lore (depicting places where the boundaries between this world and the otherworld overlap), and includes oral customs and historical records-keeping, particularly family "genealogies" and the association of illustrious ancestors with particular landmarks, in addition to "stories of conquest" (Ní Dhomhnaill 1996, 408-9). Joyce's poem can be categorised as a "typical" nature poem.[31] The lack of place-specificity in her poem helps Joyce create a timeless landscape, one wherein she presents Traveller cultural activity as integral. Her variation on the nature poem genre assumes political implications as the poem obliquely addresses those

---

[29] These (often-itinerant) oral scholars played an important role as "public intellectuals and principal advisors to the chieftains" (Flannery 1997, 18) under the Celtic system.

[30] *Dinnseanchas* is a compound word that approximately translates as Dinn, "landmark, eminent or notable place" and seanchas, "lore" (Ní Dhomhnaill 1996, 408).

[31] While Joyce's poem does not allude to any specific place or landmark, nature poems sometimes focused on a particular setting. In his essay, "The God in the Tree", Seamus Heaney quotes a translation of a fifteenth or sixteenth century Irish poem attributed by tradition to Oisin, "Benn Boilbin" (Heaney 1980, 184), that opens with the mountain made famous by W.B. Yeats's "Under Ben Bulben". Besides such place-specific nature poetry, Heaney's own translation of *Buile Suibhne* (i.e., *Sweeney Astray*), includes long passages in praise of trees that make no specific reference to place (Heaney 1980, 187-8), and instead emphasises a natural world where human activity is peripheral. The only direct references to a human presence in the quoted passage are "The yew tree in each churchyard" and "life-blood on a spear-shaft" (Heaney 1984, 188: 25, 30). The poet's voice uses metaphorical language to describe forest trees where, "some milk of human kindness / cours[es] in its sap" (Heaney 1984, 187: 7-8). Similarly, Joyce's poem diminishes the impact of human activity in the shaping of the landscape, thereby presenting a more pristine and unspoilt setting.

non-Traveller attitudes that frequently seek to eliminate all nomads from the landscape.

Her poem returns to some treasured images from her childhood, a montage of memory that incorporates both joy and sadness. As a child, she writes, though she may have been "very poor", yet her life was enriched with "a beauty that money could not buy" (Joyce 1994, 36: 4-28). Joyce rejects material possessions as a barometer for success, declaring, "No toy could give me this much happiness" (1994, 36: 19). Her observations of community activity emphasize human interaction as the catalyst for her contentment, a theme also found in other autobiographical writings by Traveller writers (see Cawley, 2004). Their material poverty contrasts with the spiritual richness proffered by the natural beauty that is the Irish landscape:

> Oh, but hadn't I all the beauty,
> That mother nature put on earth,
> The different kinds of wild flowers,
> That no one ever planted.[32] (Joyce 1994, 36: 5-8)

The role of human agency in shaping the Irish landscape by human history is explored in Joyce's autobiography, *My Life on the Road (2000*). Here, Joyce establishes the attachment of Travellers to Ireland as a geographic space through the tradition of storytelling and the tradition that is *dinnsheanchas*. Her early years had seen her father's informal education of his children and Joyce herself via the medium that is the oral transmission of historical knowledge – i.e., history as a form of storytelling. As they travelled the country, Joyce and her siblings prompted their father with many questions "about old castles or houses or monuments" (2000, 5), and he, in turn, would tell them "the history of all the places we passed through" (2000, 5). Her anecdote recalls the "fugitive" (Hayes cited in Gibbons 1996, 145) mobility of orality, oral forms – songs and storytelling – which participate through the spoken word in shared symbols. Young Nan's responsiveness to her surroundings, together with her father's knowledge of the past elicits a special narrative and suggests the active involvement that underlines the Traveller community's historic connection with the landscape. It validates the Travellers own "*dinnseanchas*"; their sense of belonging with the various camping places their families' have visited for generations. Joyce's reminiscence also points to Ireland as a place where history is perceptible

[32] The last line places a boundary between the natural world and the sphere of human activity. Human agency is absent from this wild garden.

in the very topography of the landscape, a trope which has been exploited by innumerable Irish writers[33]. Her narrative involves a relation with landscape that is set in the immediate present but one which also calls upon the past to impart meaning beyond its mere physical manifestations. Behind every rock, castle, field, and tower, there is a story, stories which are not always contained within the more "official" representations of the past, e.g., public monuments – since the latter tend to favour officially-sanctioned elements of the historical experience. Of course, Traveller *dinnsheanchas*, the narratives by which historical meaning is imparted to their community's environment, are an amalgam of both "official" and unofficial history and as in any community, represent their attempts to more accurately describe their experience of the land. As Traveller Johnny Collins (1992) asserts in *Traveller Ways, Traveller Words* (a collection of shorter autobiographies conducted as interviews), "Travellers always gev [gave] their camps their own names" (1992, 32), names derived from their own experiences of the place, and as relating to e.g., camp conditions, topography, the surnames or occupations of neighbouring "settled" people, etc. The personalization of place-names by group consent creates a sense of psychic belonging and in addition, a sense of autonomy and solidarity. As Collins (1992) notes, "The settled people'd never know the names of, iv the camps we use' ta live in" (1992, 32).

Joyce's poem blends together the important sense of history and patriotism her father imparts to the landscape and combines patriotism with an exaltation of nature in all its fullness. The language of patriotism invokes the mythologies of nationhood. The poem moves from the sweeping "beauty of Ireland" (1994, 36: 9) to the smaller locations: "The silver running streams beside the green fields, / Covered with yellow buttercups" (Joyce 1994, 36: 10, 11). The next line sees the landscape transformed into "our beloved tricolour" (Joyce 1994, 36: 12), an allusion to the green, white and gold Irish national flag. The possessive pronoun "our" claims a share in this most immediately recognizable symbol of national identity, the flag, a physical emblem of nationhood and nationalism. As an "empty signifier" (Duncan and Duncan 1992, 22), the

---

33 Traces of the "Famine roads" which lead nowhere, as built by starving peasants on a "work" programme which was part of the British colonial response to famine are poetically described in Eavan Boland's "That the Science of Cartography is Limited". Seamus Heaney's many explorations in *North*, *Field Work*, *Station Island* are other examples. In prose, Nuala O'Faolain's novel about the Irish Famine, *My Dream of You* (2001), explores the ways in which the landscape is still shaped by reminders of the Famine, including traces of the abandoned potato fields.

flag ensures that Traveller patriotism, the Irish landscape and the Traveller way of life become one within that landscape, an ineffaceable presence and a claim to belonging that is further reinforced by the preoccupations of the second half of the poem. The final section of the poem sees Joyce recalling a time-honoured Traveller tradition, the caring for and trading of horses:

> To look at father shoeing the horses,
> Paring the horses' hooves,
> Picking up the little pieces
> Then to listen to the Travelling men,
> Dealing and swapping horses,
> Trotting the horses up and down the old tat road,
> To hear the noise of their hooves. (1994, 36: 19-25)

While the actual locale is an indeterminate one, the portrayal of this occupation on an Irish byway establishes the Traveller presence firmly within the Irish landscape. (It is as if their presence is reinforced by the sound of the rhythm of horses' hooves pounding the road.) Roland Barthes (1989) claims that myth "transforms history into nature" (1989, 129). His implication is that mythology seeks to naturalize a nation's historical contingencies. Joyce's poem also transforms nature so as to encompass history, and simultaneously reshapes the Irish landscape so as to accommodate the integral presence that is the Traveller community. Whereas in *My Life on the Road* (2000), her father's history-telling re-creates a metaphorical space, a "sense" of belonging through language, Joyce's poem, "The Beauty I Can See" (1994), takes this notion one step further. Joyce's conflation of landscape, nation, and a unique community's traditions usurps "received" circumstances that have created conditions that resemble a type of "internal exile"[34]. She naturalizes a Traveller presence and history within the contours of a landscape. By employing this metaphor, Joyce insists on the Traveller community's right to an equal sense of national belonging. At its most essential, Joyce re-writes Travellers into the contours of the Irish nation.

Maher (1998), too, expresses an intimate relationship with the natural world as when he finishes his memoir with a poetic exaltation of nature's wonder. He concludes his narrative with a type of euphoria, a state of bliss achieved through the healing power of a natural world which symbolically assuages and erases the misery, isolation and despair of much of his

---

[34] This "internal exile" is largely imposed by external conditions resulting from exclusionary practices.

preceding narrative. The loneliness of the road has been a recurring theme in his life story up to this point. Now, in this moment, he intimates a profound sense of kinship with the non-human world, the world of nature's beauty:

> Even now, on this heavenly dawning day, as I tread onwards, my thoughts are beautifully distracted by the sound of God's feathered creatures bursting into morning song. How I envy the birds' joyous song; for them, sweet creatures, song is contentment, joy and happiness ... Listening and drunk with rapture, a tear and a smile come together, for I feel good at this break of a new day, heralded by a million voices of God's feathered creatures. Times like this are heaven to me, taking me into a different and more beautiful world. (1998, 163)

For Maher, the end is also a beginning. The final pages of his book describe his central character (i.e. himself) walking along a road, still unsure of his exact destination, yet moving forward towards a new day. Time conceived as a linear progression is a "Western" concept that has shaped narrative but which does not necessarily typify a life experience, especially a life lived on the periphery of society. The concept of time as circular in primary and secondary oral cultures, time as a succession of seasons and life cycles, belies the "life as a narrative" format of the classic autobiographical template. Maher's inconclusive ending conforms to the "traditional" "road" novel in many ways since it disrupts the Aristotelian longing for a dénouement. Paradoxically, as with apocalyptic thinking, the notion of heaven proposes an end that is both the end of time (the world as we know it) and a new beginning. Maher is seen reaching out to his reader, looking for connections by using the first person plural and extending the notions of human kinship when he writes, "In reality, each and every one of us is on the road" (1998, 165). By this, he suggests that all people are travellers on this same journey of life. Maher's symbol of "this earthly road" (1998, 162) points to his belief that this world is only one of many. The symbol evokes the pilgrimage motif of the early Christian Church. "[E]arthly road" points to a heavenly counterpart, as does the phrase, "Whether I shall experience [happiness] in this world, I know not" (1998, 162). In the final paragraph, the afterlife is a campsite, or "mollying ground". Maher recognizes the reader as kindred when he proposes, "one day, please God, we shall all meet at the final mollying ground" (1998, 165).

The moments of "rapture" Maher experiences in these closing pages intimate that one can experience a foretaste of "heaven" here on earth through an appreciation of nature. Maher is referring here not to the objective world which science observes and studies, but the world of

God's creation, a world where nature is still a "wonder" (1998, 163). The "dawning day" opens up new beginnings, "a new journey and only God knows what lies ahead" (1998, 163). In this conclusion, Maher is searching for hope, but his search is an ambivalent one. A profound sadness pervades his narrative, a grief at what he sees as the destruction of his own people, "the horribleness of modern ethics and thinking, a grave insult to God, the Creator of all" (1998, 164). Maher concludes his autobiography by declaring modernity to be antithetical to the Spirit.

Joyce (2000) also attempts to conclude *My Life on the Road* (originally, *Traveller* 1985) with a sense of hope, but it is as if she is attempting to convince herself as much as the reader, as if she is shoring up her own sense of courage. Her final chapter in the book mirrors her first in that she employs the collective "we". In the final paragraph of her book, this usage is more unequivocal than ever. Joyce speaks on behalf of her community and outlines the challenges which lie ahead. For Joyce, ignorance remains the greatest obstacle to "A Better Understanding", the title of her concluding chapter and indeed her penultimate sentence: "What we want most of all is a better understanding with the settled people: that we should understand them and they should understand us" (2000, 118). She notes that Travellers are now "able and willing to speak up for themselves" (2000, 118), an increase in political involvement that reflects a community growing in confidence. Joyce believes that improved access to education for Traveller children is the solution that will ensure a better future for the Traveller community. Her final chapter contains optimism ("the last few years have been a great point in the travellers' history" (2000, 118)), and hope ("I would like all the travelling children to have self-confidence and to grow up proud of what they are" (117)), but a residue of bitterness remains too: "But the way they've been treated and discriminated against they grow up ashamed of their own parents" (2000, 117). In the afterword to *Traveller*, appended fifteen years later, her hopes are tinged with a sense of resignation. Gone is some of her early optimism to be replaced by a more pragmatic analysis of the future challenges faced by the Traveller community in Ireland.

CONCLUSIONS: EXCLUSIONS

The afterword to *Traveller* (appended to *My Life on the Road*, 2000) gives an important update, one which is crucial for the perspectives it provides on the privileged speaker, and the subtlety and pervasiveness of ongoing exclusionary practices. Joyce experiences the pain of invisibility, of being overlooked not just by people who were prejudicial against Travellers but also by "settled people" who sympathized with the Traveller cause. At a time when she was travelling Ireland, campaigning for Traveller rights, appearing in the national media and running for public office, Joyce was still overlooked for paid positions in emerging Traveller organizations. "[T]he ones that got the jobs were all settled people. When the money came for the training centre, it was all settled people working there and they never said to me 'Nan, you've great experience, why don't you come in?' It wasn't for the sake of money, but it was making a person a full person" (Joyce 2000, xi). Her supposed ineligibility for these jobs in spite of her capabilities and life experience points to the undervaluing of certain types of knowledge that assigns an inferior status to experience, in particular. Joyce's supposed "ineligibility" for these positions also underlines the self-perpetuation of privilege as encompassed within a third-level education. Functioning at a more unconscious level, the inculcation of unspoken codes of behaviour and societal values which favour the privileged combine to construct a framework for in-group / out-group relations whereby societal groups maintain "boundaries". Just as harmful as overt racism are such exclusionary practices by more privileged groups[1], practices which are so internalized as relating to the maintenance of group "norms" that they need not even be justified in the form of words. Codes of silence prevail that effect the perpetuation of discriminatory practices based not only on race, but also class and cultural distinctions (identifiable through accent, idiom, decorum and attire), and religious / cultural differences, especially where the latter are expressed as visible symbols.

---

[1] Dividing practices are generally reciprocal in nature. However, because more privileged groups wield more influence and power while marginalized groups tend to be more vulnerable, the negative effects of exclusionary practices are more likely to be felt by the latter.

Joyce describes situations where she was made to feel dependent. She begins by contrasting her economic situation with "those" non-Travellers sympathetic to the Traveller cause. She insists that her grievances in no way relate to the disparity between their economic situations, but she cannot accept the humiliation of being made to feel dependent on others. As she travelled around the country to speak, Joyce explains, "[T]hose would be driving around in their big cars and their expenses … those would be driving me in the car and I'd be in the back and they'd have their cheque books and if you got hungry you'd have to wait for them to go into a café and buy you a coffee or a sandwich" (2000, xii). Joyce juxtaposes emblems of dependency and independence where driving a car is symbolic of being in control of one's itinerary and the back seat is for the passengers. The passengers are those "dependents" who must wait for the decisions of others while the person who holds the chequebook represents the one who controls the finances. She feels herself reduced to a child-like status. While there is no suggestion of any malice on the part of these non-Traveller supporters, there is certainly evidence of some degree of insensitivity. As if in reciprocation for being made to feel a "non-person", Joyce inverts the power relationship by placing her words in the mouths of those she feels "controlled" by: "You go around, doing great work, and people say 'go ahead and we'll take the benefit of the work'" (2000, xi). Joyce's experience demonstrates that when hitherto "silenced" people begin to speak on their own behalf, they can encounter "resistance" in the form of entrenched or authoritative positions that construe their informal knowledge base as "inadequate to the task". Similarly, when more sophisticated academic discourses promote theoretical frameworks which question the validity of non-theoretical knowledge such as "the language of experience," the tendency to dismiss such forms of knowledge can be expressed in "sophisticated" ways and yet represents an exclusionary practice.

CONCLUSION / INCLUSION

What does the future hold for Travellers? Sibley (1995) contends that assimilationist policies fail because governments underestimate "the capacity of the minority to resist and to maintain its own cultural values" (1995, 84). As based on the texts examined here, Traveller writing / orality tends to support Sibley's assertion. However, Joyce's (2000) bittersweet afterword to her autobiography highlights the ongoing nature of the struggle. Even as she celebrates the increased confidence "of traveller women coming out and speaking for themselves" (2000, xv) and finds a new hope in the younger generation, she concludes with an uncharacteristic pessimism, observing, "still there's a lot of hatred, some people have this hatred and I don't think they'll ever get rid of it" (2000, xv). This more "resigned" voice reflects perhaps Joyce's withdrawal from her more public life as an activist, and evokes Homi Bhabha's idea of the limited yet significant role of the storyteller, one who offers "no salvation, but a strange cultural survival of the people" (1994, 170). For minority "voices" speaking from the peripheries, every battle is hard-fought, the conclusions are never certain, and more often than not, they simply herald the prelude to the next struggle.

As Joyce has anticipated, access to education remains key to developing Traveller pride and autonomy. Having received an MA in Ethnic and Racial Studies from Trinity College Dublin, Traveller activist and playwright Rosaleen McDonagh's third-level education still makes her a minority among Travellers. Her original "one-woman show depicting the social care system for Travellers in the 1960s and 70s" ("Rosaleen" 15), *The Baby Doll Project*, first staged in Dublin, January 2003 tackles issues of racism and attitudes towards the physically challenged (McDonagh has cerebral palsy). More recently, she has staged a "reworked reading" of a play in progress, *John and Josie* that, in her explorations of sexual orientation and non-traditional families, opens up new directions in Traveller self-identities[1]. Because music and theatre integrate the orality of performance, as de Certeau observes, they represent "a space where the organizing power of reason is effaced" (1988, 183),

[1] *Editor's note*: McDonagh's work remains controversial and is not widely accepted by Travellers themselves.

and where the "recalcitrance" of oral cultural expressions find voice. Writing in genres which preserve the power of language as spoken word – i.e., genres such as poetry, storytelling and song – may be one of the most powerful tools of resistance to assimilationist pressures for Travellers. The transformative and regenerative qualities of poetry and its plays of meaning are particularly resistant[2] to appropriation into dominant discourses. Traveller efforts to reshape hegemonic representations and reinvent categories of discourse are ongoing and in response to changing conditions.

Rather than dismiss Traveller representations as naïve, a move which only reiterates exclusionary practices, academics and citizens must listen seriously and respectfully to what these representations say or do not say, how they work and what they are attempting to do, remembering always that in autobiography, these rhetorical strategies represent an individual person's dignity and life experience. Searching for common ground between communities, Maher declares that we are all fellow travellers on the same road. His oblique reference to a future life (or afterlife) admonishes us to consider where that road leads, not only for Travellers, but also for the people of the nation-state as a whole. Proponents of saner development policies in Ireland and abroad, including ecologists and environmentalists are increasingly highlighting the fact that certain values are lacking in the modern ethos. As a consequence, they have begun to listen to those voices that recount stories based on the oral tradition, stories imbued with mystery, and stories wherein human beings understand their vulnerability and the limitations of the human condition. This admission of finiteness allows for a new humility, one which acknowledges that all of existence shares the same origins and the same destiny to some degree. This dialogic aspect of orality may be better positioned to provide a more holistic approach towards ecological health precisely because it views the earth's problems as interconnected in nature. Similarly, the conflicting demands between both indigenous and nomadic peoples, and developers and conservationists are unlikely to be resolved except through intensive democratic debate at the grassroots level, i.e., individual struggle by individual struggle. This is because, as Travellers are acutely aware, land-use is a highly-politicized issue and arbitration tends to favour the more influential interest groups.

---

[2] This observation holds true only if there is no apparent market value inherent in that particular form of artistic expression. The all-engulfing capitalist credo of, "If it sells, use it," always must apply. In "Mapping the Postmodern", Huyssen (1990) cites counter-cultural movements that are then appropriated into the "mainstream" as a signal for the demise of modernism.

What of Traveller traditions? Joyce's sister, Chrissie Ward observes that in the days of her childhood, "the roads was narrower but the land was wider" (1992, 46). (She is referring here to the unused land on either side of the road where Travellers could once pull in, in order to camp.) Today, in contemporary Ireland as elsewhere, the land has grown "narrower" – i.e., it is more divided, fenced in and set apart for specific use by property owners. Today land is a limited commodity, and is therefore more crowded and less available for informal use. A Commission of the European Community Synthesis Report, "School Provision for Gypsy and Traveller Children" published in 1987, optimistically put forward that Travellers will never disappear because "'*[n]omadism is as much a state of mind as a state of fact*'" (italics in McDonagh, cited in McDonagh 1994, 96). This Report seems to argue that nomadism is "subjective" and involves "*feeling* oneself to be a Traveller" (my italics, McDonagh 1994, 96). This is undoubtedly true, as verified by Traveller autobiographies (see Cawley 2004; Dunne 2004), and represents one of the ways Travellers have employed to redefine their identity. At the same time, the tendency for literate thinking to render concrete realities as abstractions underlies this statement which, despite its optimism, seems to transform "the objective reality of travelling" (McDonagh 1994, 96) to a more subjective abstraction which fails to address the long-term damage induced by anti-nomadic policies. In point of fact, the gradual move away from tradition (recorded in an array of Traveller autobiographies) has meant that Travellers, like many other minorities, have also had to redefine themselves – to themselves.

Writing orality, performance and social activism all represent discursive strategies of resistance which provide catalysts for the emergence of new and diverse Traveller self-identities. Reading and writing the oral tradition reveals the reality whereby subjugated knowledges sometimes run parallel to, exist outside of, or traverse more officially-sanctioned ways of speaking. Traveller perspectives help to connect with those gaps in our cultural knowledge. They challenge our complacency and broaden our awareness of other modes of living, being, and narrating our lives.

WORKS CITED

"Background to the Irish Conflict." *Irelandseye.com.* <http://www.irelandseye.com/aarticles/history/events/conflict/bttc1.shtm>. 14 November 2007.

Barthes, Roland. *Mythologies.* Trans. Annette Lavers. New York: Farrar, Straus & Giroux, 1989.

Bhabha, Homi. *The Location of Culture*. London & New York: Routledge, 1994.

Blondin, George. *When the World Was New: Stories of the Sahtú Dene*. Yellowknife: Outcrop, The Northern Publishers, 1990.

Bloy, Marjie. "The Irish Famine: 1845-9." *The Victorian Web*. 11 October 2002. <http://www.victorianweb.org/history/famine.html>. 26 June 2006.

Boland, Eavan. "The Colonists." *The Lost Land*. New York & London: W.W. Norton, 1998. 8-9.

—. "Lava Cameo." *In a Time of Violence*. Manchester : Carcanet, 1994. 35-6.

Bourke, Angela. "The Virtual Reality of Irish Fairy Legend." *Éire-Ireland*. 31.1 & 2 (1996): 7-25.

—. "Reading in a Woman's Death: Colonial Text and Oral Tradition in Nineteenth-Century Ireland." *Feminist Studies*. 21.3 (1995): 553-586. Literature Online. Proquest. Concordia University Libraries. <http.//www.proquest.com>. 12 January 2006.

Campbell, Maria. *Half-breed*. Halifax, N.S.: Goodread Biographies, 1973.

Casey, Edward S. *Spirit and Soul: Essays in Philosophical Psychology*. Dallas: Spring Publications, 1991.

Cavallaro, Dani. *Critical and Cultural Theory: Thematic Variations*. London & New Brunswick, NJ: Athlone P, 2001.

Cawley, William. *The Candlelight Painter: The Life and Work of William Cawley, Traveller, Painter and Poet*. Ed. Mícheál Ó hAodha. Dublin: A & A Farmar, 2004.

Chew, Robin. 10 September 2007. "Adam Smith: Philosopher." *Lucidcafé.* <http://www.lucidcafe.com/library/96jun/smith.html>. 1 October 2007.

Collins, Johnny. *Traveller Ways, Traveller Words*. Ed. Gearóid Ó Riain. Dublin: Pavee Point, 1992. 32-41.

Condren, Mary. *The Serpent and the Goddess: Women, Religion and Power in Celtic Ireland*. New York: Harper and Row, 1989.

Cruikshank, Julie. "Notes and Comments: Oral Tradition and Oral History – Reviewing Some Issues." *The Canadian Historical Review*. 75.3 (1994): 403. Proquest. Concordia University Libraries. <http://www.proquest.com>. 16 November 2005.

—. *The Social Life of Stories*. Vancouver: UBC Press, 1998.

Cusack, George. "The Playboy of the Western World." *The Literary Encyclopedia*. 26 November 2004. <http://www.litencyc.com/php/sworks.php?rec=true&UID=10167>. 28 January 2007.

De Certeau, Michel. *The Writing of History*. Trans. Tom Conley. New York: Columbia UP, 1988.

Delaney, Paul. "Stories from Below: Seán Maher and Nan Joyce." 32-40. *The Stranger in Ourselves: Ireland's Others*. Ed. Mícheál Ó hAodha, David O'Donnell and Colm Power. Dublin: A & A Farmar, 2006. 32-40.

Duncan, James S. and Nancy G. Duncan. "Ideology and Bliss: Roland Barthes and the Secret Histories of Landscape." *Writing Worlds: Discourse, Text and Metaphor in the Representation of Landscape*. Ed. Trevor J. Barnes & James S. Duncan. London & New York: Routledge, 1992.

Dunne, Pecker. *Parley Poet and Chanter: A Life of Pecker Dunne*. Ed. Mícheál Ó hAodha. Dublin: A & A Farmar, 2004.

Dyer, Richard. *Images: Essays on Representations*. London & New York: Routledge, 1993.

Eagleton, Terry. *The Illusions of Postmodernism*. Oxford & Cambridge, MS: Blackwell, 1997.

—. *Ideology: An Introduction*. London & New York: Verso, 1991.

Eakin, Paul John. *How Our Lives Become Stories: Making Selves*. Ithaca, NY: Cornell UP, 1999.

Eliade, Mircea. *Myths, Dreams and Mysteries: The Encounter between Contemporary Faiths and Archaic Realities*. New York: Harper & Row, 1967.

—. *The Sacred and the Profane*. Trans. Willard R. Trask. Harcourt, Brace & World, New York: 1959.

Eyerman, Ron. *Cultural Trauma: Slavery and the Formation of African American Identity*. Cambridge: Cambridge UP, 2001.

Farmar, Anna. E-mail to the author. December 13, 2005.

Felman, Shoshana. "Madness and Philosophy or Literature's Reason." *Yale French Studies*. 52. (1975): 206-28.

Finan, Thomas. "Hiberno-Latin Christian Literature." *An Introduction to Celtic Christianity*. Ed. James P. Mackey. Edinburgh: T & T Clark, 1989. 64-100.

Flannery, James W. *Dear Harp of My Country: The Irish Melodies of Thomas Moore*. Nashville: J.S. Sanders, 1997.

Flax, Jane. *Thinking Fragments: Psychoanalysis, Feminism, and Postmodernism in the Contemporary West*. Berkeley, Los Angeles & Oxford: U of California P, 1990.

Fowler, Robert M. "How the Secondary Orality of the Electronic Age Can Awaken Us to the Primary Orality of Antiquity or What Hypertext Can Teach Us About the Bible with Reflections on the Ethical and Political Issues of the Electronic Frontier." <http://homepages.bw.edu/~rfowler/pubs/secondoral/index.html>. 16 October 2006.

Foucault, Michel. *Abnormal: Lectures at the Collège de France, 1974-1975*. London & New York: Verso, 2003.

—. *The History of Sexuality: Volume I: An Introduction*. Trans. Robert Hurley. New York: Vintage, 1988.

—. "Truth and Power." *Power/Knowledge: Selected Interviews and Other Writings, 1972-1977*. Ed. & Trans. Colin Gordon. New York: Pantheon, 1980. 109-133.

—. "Two Lectures." *Power/Knowledge: Selected Interviews and Other Writings, 1972-1977*. Ed. & Trans. Colin Gordon. New York: Pantheon, 1980. 78-108.

—. *Discipline and Punish*. Trans. Alan Sheridan. New York: First Vintage, 1979.

—. *Madness and Civilization: A History of Insanity in the Age of Reason*. Trans. Richard Howard. London: Tavistock, 1965.

Fraser, Nancy. *Unruly Practices: Power, Discourse and Gender in Contemporary Social Theory*. Cambridge, UK: Polity Press, 1989.

Friedman, Susan Stanford. "Women's Autobiographical Selves: Theory and Practice." *The Private Self: Theory and Practice of Women's Autobiographical Writings.* Ed. Shari Benstock. Chapel Hill and London: U of North Carolina P, 1988. 34-62.

Gaffey, Bridget. Preface. *Moving Stories: Traveller Women Write*. Southwark Traveller Women's Group. London: Traveller Education Team, 1992. 8-9.

Garrard, Greg. *Ecocriticism*. London & New York: Routledge, 2004.

Gibbons, Luke. *Transformations in Irish Culture*. Cork: Cork UP, 1996.

Gilmore, Leigh. *Autobiographics: A Feminist Theory of Women's Self-Representation*. Ithaca: Cornell UP, 1994.

Gray, Peter. *Psychology*. 2nd Edition. New York: Worth Publishers, 1994.

Gray, Peter. *The Irish Famine*. New York: Harry N. Abrams, 1995.

Green, Miranda J. *The World of the Druids*. London: Thames and Hudson, 1997.

Gregory, Lady. *A Book of Saints and Wonders Put Down Here by Lady Gregory According to the Old Writings and the Memory of the People of Ireland*. New York: Oxford UP, 1971.

Greyson, Bruce and Mitchell B. Liester. "Auditory Hallucinations Following Near-Death Experiences." *Journal of Humanistic Psychology*. 44. 3 (2004): 320-336.

Habermas, Jürgen. *The Philosophical Discourse of Modernity: Twelve Lectures*. Trans. Frederick Lawrence. Cambridge: Polity P, 1987.

Hanson, R.P.C. "The Mission of Saint Patrick." *An Introduction to Celtic Christianity*. Ed. James P. Mackey. Edinburgh: T & T Clark, 1989. 22-44.

Hardiman, Niamh, Tony McCashin & Diane Payne. "Understanding Irish Attitudes to Poverty & Wealth." Dublin: Institute for the Study of Social Change, 2004. (Now the Geary Institute). Now published in *Irish Social and Political Attitudes*. Ed. John Garry, Niamh Hardiman & Diane Payne. Liverpool: Liverpool UP, 2006.

Hayes, Michael. *Irish Travellers: Representations and Realities*. Dublin: Liffey, 2006.

Hayes, Tom. "Diggers, Ranters, and Women Prophets: The Discourse of Madness and the Cartesian Cogito in Seventeenth-Century England." *CLIO: A Journal of Literature, History, and the Philosophy of History*. 26. 1(1996): 29-50. Literature Online. Proquest. Concordia University Libraries. <http.//www.proquest.com>. 9 April 2006.

Heaney, Seamus. *Sweeney Astray*. London & Boston: Faber and Faber, 1984.

—. "The God in the Tree: Early Irish Nature Poetry." *Preoccupations: Selected Prose: 1968-1978*. New York: Farrar, Straus and Giroux, 1980.

Hearne, Dana. Lecture. Irish Nationalisms. Concordia University, Montreal, QC. March 22, 2006.

Heilbrun, Carolyn G. "Non-Autobiographies of 'Privileged' Women: England and America." *Life / Lines: Theorizing Women's Autobiography*. Ed. Bella Brodzki and Celeste Schenck. Ithaca and London: Cornell UP, 1988. 62-76.

Helleiner, Jane. *Irish Travellers: Racism and the Politics of Culture*. Toronto: U of Toronto P, 2000.

Herr, Cheryl Temple. *The Field*. Cork: Cork UP, 2002.

Hirschmann, Nancy J. *The Subject of Liberty: Toward a Feminist Theory of Freedom*. Princeton & Oxford: Princeton UP, 2003.

Hughes, Christina. *Key Concepts in Feminist Theory and Research*. London, Thousand Oaks, CA & New Delhi: Sage, 2002.

Huyssen, Andreas. "Mapping the Postmodern." *Feminism / Postmodernism*. Ed. Linda J. Nicholson. London & New York: Routledge, 1990. 234-277.

Johansen, Bruce. *Forgotten Founders: How the American Indian Helped Shape Democracy*. Boston: Harvard Common P, 1987. <http://www.ratical.org/many_worlds/6Nations/FF.html>. 28 March 2007.

"John and Josie." <http://www.dublinks.com/index.cfm/loc/14/pt/0/spid/3ED53A1F-AB93-4DC9-936617F06D2A98B7.htm>. 02 February 2007.

Johnston, Wesley. "Prelude to Famine 2 : Thc Potato." *Ireland's Great Famine : 1845-1849*. <http://www.wesleyjohnston.com/users/ireland/past/famine/potato.html>. 23 February 2006.

Jovanovic, Pierre. *L'enquête sur l'existence des anges gardiens*. Paris: France Loisirs, 1993.

Joyce, Catherine. Presenter. 2002. "Report to the Anti-Poverty Learning Network Combat Poverty Agency." *Irish Traveller Movement*. <http://www.itmtrav.com/publications/ReportAntiPoverty02.html>. 16 Nov. 2006.

Joyce, Nan. *My Life on the Road*. Ed. Anna Farmar. Dublin: A. & A. Farmar, 2000. Formerly *Traveller*. Dublin: Gill and Macmillan, 1985.

—. "The Beauty I Can See." *Blackstones Around the Green Shamrock: A Poetry Anthology By and About Travellers*. Ed. O'Reilly, Michael and Máirín Kenny. Blackrock Teachers' Centre, 1994. 36.

Kadar, Marlene. "The Devouring: Traces of Roma in the Holocaust: No Tattoo, Sterilized Body, Gypsy Girl." *Tracing the Autobiographical*. Ed. Marlene Kadar, Linda Warley, Jeanne Perrault & Susanna Egan. Waterloo: Wilfred Laurier UP, 2005. 223-46.

Keane, John B. *The Field*. Dublin & Cork: Mercier P, 1980.

Kennedy, Liam. *Colonialism, Religion and Nationalism in Ireland*. Belfast: Queen's U of Belfast, 1996.

Keeshig-Tobias, Lenore. "Stop Stealing Native Stories." *The Globe and Mail*. 26 Jan. 1990: A7.

Laing, Elizabeth. Introduction. *Moving Stories: Traveller Women Write*. Southwark Traveller Women's Group. London: Traveller Education Team, 1992. 6-7.

Lanham, Richard A. *A Handlist of Rhetorical Terms*. Berkeley, Los Angeles & London: U of California P, 1991.

Lanters, José. "'We are a Different People': Life Writing, Representation, and the Travellers." *New Hibernia Review Iris Éireannach Nua*. 9. 2(2005): 25-41.

Laughlin, Jim Mac. "Nation-Building, Social Closure and Anti-Traveller Racism in Ireland." *Sociology*. 33. 1(1999): 129-151.

—. *Travellers and Ireland: Whose Country, Whose History?* Cork: Cork UP, 1995.

Lee, Ronald. *Goddam Gypsy: An Autobiographical Novel.* Montreal, Tundra: 1971.

Lockett, Christopher. "Terror and Rebirth: Cathleen ní Houlihan, from Yeats to the Crying Game." *Literature Film Quarterly*. 2005. Find Articles. Proquest. <http://findarticles.com/p/articles/mi_qa3768/is_200510/ai_n15957566/pg_1>. 10 April 2007.

Mackenzie, Shelagh. Dir. *Remember Africville*. National Film Board of Canada, 1991.

Maher, Sean. *The Road to God Knows Where: A Memoir of a Travelling Boyhood*. Dublin: Veritas, 1998. Originally Talbot Press, 1972.

Malpas, Jeff. "Hans-Georg Gadamer." 1 August 2005. *Stanford Encyclopedia of Philosophy*. <http://plato.stanford.edu/entries/gadamer/>. 1 October 2007.

Mason, Mary G. "The Other Voice: Autobiographies of Women Writers." *Life / Lines:Theorizing Women's Autobiography*. Ed. Bella Brodzki and Celeste Schenck. Ithaca and London: Cornell UP, 1988. 19-44.

Matas, Robert. Erin Anderssen, and Sean Fine. "Natives Win on Land Rights: Top Court Rules that Oral History Gives Bands Constitutional Claim in Absence of Treaties." 12 Dec. 1997. <http://www.hartford-hwp.com/archives/41/343.html>. 16 November 2006.

McCormack, Joseph. "The Black and Tans." 1986. <http://www.irish-society.org/Hedgemaster%20Archives/black-tans.htm>. 8 October 2007.

McDonagh, Kathleen. *Moving Stories: Traveller Women Write*. Southwark Traveller Women's Group. London: Traveller Education Team, 1992. 49-53.

McDonagh, Michael. "Nomadism in Irish Travellers' Identity." *Irish Travellers: Culture and Ethnicity*. Ed. May McCann, Séamas Ó Síocháin & Joseph Ruane. Belfast: Institute of Irish Studies, The Queen's University of Belfast, 1994. 95-109.

McLoughlin, Dympna. "Ethnicity and Irish Travellers: Reflections on Ní Shúinéar." *Irish Travellers: Culture and Ethnicity*. Ed. May McCann, Séamas, Ó Síocháin & Joseph Ruane. Belfast: Institute of Irish Studies, The Queen's University of Belfast, 1994. 78-94.

McVeigh, Robbie. "Theorising Sedentarism: The Roots of Anti-Nomadism." *Gypsy Politics and Traveller Identity*. Ed. Thomas Acton. Hertfordshire: U of Hertfordshire P, 1997. 7-25.

McVeigh, Robbie and Ronit Lentin. "Situated Racisms: A Theoretical Introduction." *Racism and Anti- racism in Ireland*. Ed. Ronit Lentin & Robbie McVeigh. Belfast: Beyond the Pale, 2002. 1-48.

"The Merchants of Cool." *Frontline*. PBS. 27 February 2001.

Merriman, Victor. "Decolonisation Postponed: The Theatre of Tiger Trash." *Irish University Review*. 29. 2(1999): 305-317.

Morgan, Hiram. "Ulster Plantation." Microsoft Encarta Online Encyclopedia. 2007. <http://uk.encarta.msn.com/ encyclopedia_761580221/Ulster_Plantation.html>. 14 November 2007.

"Myths, Hypotheses and Facts Concerning the Origin of Peoples: The True Origin of Roma and Sinti: Map." <http://www.imninalu.net/Roma_map.htm>. 23 February 2006.

Ní Dhomhnaill, Nuala. "Dinnsheanchas: The Naming of High or Holy Places." *The Geography of Identity*. Ed. Patricia Yaeger. Ann Arbor: The U of Michigan P, 1996. 408-432.

Ní Shuinéar, Sinéad. "Othering the Irish (Travellers)." *Racism and Anti-racism in Ireland*. Ed. Ronit Lentin & Robbie McVeigh. Belfast: Beyond the Pale, 2002. 177-192.

—. "Irish Travellers, Ethnicity and the Origins Question." *Irish Travellers: Culture and Ethnicity*. Ed. May McCann, Séamas Ó Síocháin & Joseph Ruane. Belfast: Institute of Irish Studies, The Queen's University of Belfast, 1994. 54-77.

O'Donoghue, Noel Dermot. *The Angels Keep Their Ancient Places: Reflections of Celtic Spirituality*. Edinburgh & New York: T & T Clark, 2001.

—. "St. Patrick's Breastplate." *An Introduction to Celtic Christianity*. Ed. James P. Mackey. Edinburgh: T & T Clark, 1989. 45-63.

Ó Duinn, Seán. *Where Three Streams Meet: Celtic Spirituality*. Blackrock, Co. Dublin: Columba Press, 2000.

Okely, Judith. *The Traveller-Gypsies*. Cambridge: Cambridge UP, 1983.

Ong, Walter J. *Orality and Literacy: The Technologizing of the Word*. London & New York: Routledge, 1991.

—. *The Presence of the Word: Some Prolegomena for Cultural and Religious History*. New Haven & London: Yale UP, 1967.

Orr, David W. *The Nature of Design: Ecology, Culture, and Human Intention*. Oxford & New York: Oxford UP, 2002.

Pašeta, Senia. *Modern Ireland: A Very Short Introduction*. Oxford: Oxford UP, 2003.

Pierson, Ruh Roach. "Experience, Difference, Dominance and Voice in the Writing of Canadian Women's History." *Writing Women's History: International Perspectives*. Ed. Karen Offen, Ruth Roach Pierson & Jane Rendall. Bloomington: Indiana UP, 1991. 79-105.

"The Plantation of Ulster." <http://www.mccaskie.org.uk/Plantation.htm>. 23 February 2006.

Rakow, Lana F. and Laura A. Wackwitz. "Representation in Feminist Communication Theory." *Feminist Communication Theory*. Ed. Lana F. Rakow & Laura A. Wackwitz. Thousand Oaks, CA & London: Sage, 2004.

"Rosaleen." *Changing Ireland*. 12-15. *National Consulative Committee on Racism and Interculturalism*. <http://www.nccri.ie/pdf/ ChangingIrelandStories2.pdf>. 1 February 2007.

Salerno, Roger A. *Landscapes of Abandonment: Capitalism, Modernity, and Estrangement*. Albany, NY: State U of New York, 2003.

Sass, Louis A. "The Consciousness Machine: Self and Subjectivity in Schizophrenia and Modern Culture." *The Conceptual Self in Context: Culture, Experience, Self-understanding*. Ed. Ulric Neisser, David A. Jopling. Cambridge, New York & Melbourne: Cambridge UP, 1997. 203-230.

Sheridan, Jim, writer & dir. *The Field*. Perf. Sean Bean, Tom Berenger, Jenny Conroy, Brenda Fricker, Richard Harris, and Frances Tomelty. 1990. VHS. Live Home Video, 1991.

Sibley, David. *Geographies of Exclusion: Society and Difference in the West.* London & New York: Routledge, 1995.

Siegel, Kristi. *Women's Autobiographies, Culture, Feminism*. New York: Peter Lang, 2001.

Stone-Mediatore, Shari. *Reading Across Borders: Storytelling and Knowledges of Resistance*. New York & Hampshire, England: Palgrave Macmillan, 2003.

Suzuki, David. "A Personal Foreword: The Value of Native Ecologies." *Wisdom of the Elders: Honoring Sacred Native Visions of Nature*. New York and Toronto: Bantam, 1992. xxvii-xliv.

Suzuki, David with Amanda McConnell. *The Sacred Balance: Rediscovering Our Place in Nature*. Vancouver: Douglas & McIntyre, 1997.

Suzuki, David and Peter Knudtson. *Wisdom of the Elders: Honoring Sacred Native Visions of Nature*. New York and Toronto: Bantam, 1992.

Synge, John Millington. "The Tinker's Wedding." *The Playboy of the Western World and Other Plays*. Ed. Ann Saddlemyer. Oxford and New York: Oxford UP, 1998.

"Traveller Community: The History of Irish Travellers." *National Consultative Committee on Racism and Interculturalism*. <http://www.nccri.com/cdsu-travellers.html>. 22 February 2005.

"Travellers in Ireland: An Examination of Discrimination and Racism: Part 3." *Pavee Point Travellers Centre*. <http://www.paveepoint.ie/pav_irerac_3.html>. 22 February 2005.

Ward, Chrissie. "Chrissie Ward." *Traveller Ways.Traveller Words*. Ed. Gearóid Ó Riain. Dublin: Pavee Point, 1992. 42-63.

"Who We Are: Recent History." *Gitxsan Chiefs' Office*. <http://www.gitxsan.com/html/who/people/history.htm>. 16 November 2006.